PERSPECTIVE

CHUCK D. PIERCE

CHARISMA HOUSE

PERSPECTIVE by Chuck D. Pierce
Published by Charisma House, an imprint of Charisma Media
1150 Greenwood Blvd., Lake Mary, Florida 32746

While the author has made every effort to provide accurate, up-to-date source information at the time of publication, statistics and other data are constantly updated. Neither the publisher nor the author assumes any responsibility for errors or for changes that occur after publication. Further, the publisher and author do not have any control over and do not assume any responsibility for third-party websites or their content.

For more resources like this, visit MyCharismaShop.com and the author's website at gloryofzion.org.

Cataloging-in-Publication Data is on file with the Library of Congress.
International Standard Book Number: 978-1-62999-995-1
E-book ISBN: 978-1-62999-996-8

1 2025
Printed in the United States of America

Most Charisma Media products are available at special quantity discounts for bulk purchase for sales promotions, premiums, fundraising, and educational needs. For details, call us at (407) 333-0600 or visit our website at charismamedia.com.

CONTENTS

CHAPTER 1
THE NEED TO *SEE*

I HAVE WRITTEN MANY books. Some predict the future, while others elaborate on how to live a better life. Many are linked to the conflict and chaos that are part of our atmosphere and daily lives. I wrote those books in the hopes of helping people maneuver through life's valleys and mountains. This book has not been the easiest to write. When I was first commissioned to delve into how we should view our future, we were amid a pandemic, in a rapidly changing and chaotic world.

To gain perspective about our future and express with clarity *how I see* the future and *what I am seeing* for the days ahead, I needed to wait. When the waiting time was complete, the writing time followed, with some real questions in mind—among them several fundamental questions that I hope to answer: How do you see life? How do you see yourself? How do you stay focused on your path of life? Where are you going, and what will become of you?

Life is synonymous with movement. How we see ourselves in the movement all around us is key to how we live. With circumstances moving and changing so rapidly, helping you see better is essential. You *need* to see, and seeing yourself whole is most important. Even if you do not always feel OK in this changing world, *you can still be whole*! How you embrace and care for your physical, mental, and emotional well-being is essential. So is the way in which you develop your inward spirit to become strong. While you resist the swirling, chaotic atmosphere that is trying

1

to overtake you, engage in activities that produce joy. This is how you abound amid life's stresses.

VIEWPOINTS AND OPINIONS

I have always respected other people's viewpoints and opinions. My childhood was not peaceful, and I listened carefully, trying to understand how other family members viewed our difficulties. In addition, my school years coincided with a tumultuous time of war and racial tension. As my school became racially integrated, I served our student body and desired to see how other students perceived this change. Later, in the business world, I was among the pioneers of the discipline now called *human resources*. I served in several key capacities in the oil, gas, and real estate industries. In ministry I have served key leaders throughout the body of Christ and have been honored to travel the nations and see how people live all over the world.

These life experiences have shown me that people are truly interesting. My various roles have encouraged me to recognize people's perspectives, including how they view their situations and process their environments. Even after forty-plus years of ministry, I still find people interesting. They are what my life is about—the individuals, families, widows, orphans, and people of all tribes and races. The ways in which they portray their identities and belief systems shape our world.

A person's viewpoint—the "position or perspective from which something is considered or evaluated"[1]—reveals their thinking processes. You often find people with opposite viewpoints that shape their way of perceiving situations spiritually, politically, and morally. Their lives portray the perspectives that determine how they move in certain arenas and cultures and how they plow through the trials they face.

Our individual viewpoints are formed from our past, present, and future experiences and influenced by whatever we esteem as the highest level of authority in our lives. In my case I have desired my perspective to be developed through faith in the God that I've come to know. I met His Son and embraced His Spirit; therefore, my perspective has developed around the absolute authority of His Word. When He came to earth as Jesus of Nazareth, His actions presented a model of how I was to act. I have tried to be authentic in following Him as my prototype.

My life—like yours—has included many circumstances, many people, and much history. All of them have contributed to my present life. My goal is not to change your perspective but to help you see how I have learned to see, which will perhaps influence how you choose to develop your own perspective.

PERSPECTIVE AND FUTURE

Perspective and *future*: These words are the keys to understanding the changing world in which we live. *Perspective* has to do with how we see something. *Future* has to do with an expectation of some event that is yet to occur. In a world that seems to be spinning out of control, how we see and expect better days ahead becomes integral to either our well-being or our downfall.

Based on its root, the word *perspective* means to "look through."[2] How do you look at a glass containing liquid? Do you see the glass half empty or half full? Do you see through rose-colored glasses, a glass darkly (1 Cor. 13:12, KJV), a kaleidoscope, a stained glass window, or a magnifying glass? Are you viewing from the ground floor or through a clear window with a high vantage point? Your viewpoint shapes your perspective.

Situations aren't always what they seem. They might look a certain way, but when you see them from another angle, they seem to change. One approach I purposely use is sitting in different places in my home, office, restaurants, or wherever I go. I make a point of entering buildings or shopping malls through various doors, because always using the same door means seeing only certain parts of the place. Therefore, I make a very conscious effort to see the whole—whether it is in a person, place, corporate body, or nation.

Perspective is like the glass through which you view an object. When you see something three-dimensional and then draw it, you capture on a two-dimensional plane what you perceived in three-dimensional space. You can draw an object from one-, two-, three-, or even multidimensional viewpoints. Your perspective can capture a true representation of the object, or it can record how your eyes perceive it.

RECENTLY IN A PRAYER MEETING, I HEARD THE SPIRIT OF THE LORD SAY, "MY PEOPLE HAVE LOST THEIR PERSPECTIVE. THEREFORE, THEY ARE LOSING REALITY."

When several objects are grouped together or several situations happen at one time, impressions form in your mind. From what you see, you hopefully gain knowledge about how to navigate those groupings or situations. You rely on your past experiences, present knowledge, and a higher knowledge that you may never have brought fully into your situations. But as events unfold, various emotions and stimuli affect you and can cloud your way of seeing the world.

A *perspective* can also be like a trompe l'oeil painting that you see in gardens or at the end of an alley. The painting alters the space, giving a real but deceptive sense of something that is unreal. Likewise, our perspectives can seem convincing yet be inaccurate. Recently in a prayer meeting, I heard the Spirit of the Lord say, "My people have lost their perspective. Therefore, they are losing reality."

Because we can be deceived, perspective is of the utmost importance. Life itself is like a canvas with an ever-changing perspective and a horizon line. What at first seems imposing and unconquerable is often quite small and manageable when we see it from the standpoint of reality. When this happens, we realize that we initially perceived the situation through a convincing but distorted perspective.

Distorted perspectives are common to humanity. Therefore, I consider situations from the perspectives of others, including my adversaries. Yes, you and I have enemies, including an ultimate enemy that is set against life and seeks to distort how we see it.

That enemy strives to make every looming problem seem much larger than it is. In other words, he tries to frame our perspective.

We must learn how to stand back and refocus on the canvas that is life. So to accurately understand what you see, determine both your horizon line—the farthest point that you can see—and your perspective, or vantage point. Changes to either determine how and what you see. In the following sections, you will learn how important the past, present, and future are in understanding how you see life and "look through" events and issues to develop your future.

Whatever is happening, be encouraged. During dark times God encouraged His people through the prophet Jeremiah, saying, "There is a door of hope for your future after all, your children will return to their homeland" (Jer. 31:17, TPT). No matter what your current circumstances are, a door of hope is always ahead!

SEEING IN TIME AND DEVELOPING OUR BEST IDENTITY

"Jesus Christ is the same yesterday, today, and forever" (Heb. 13:8), and we are created in His image (Gen. 1:27). Although God isn't in time as we are, we live in the same three dimensions of time that Hebrews 13:8 mentions: past (yesterday), present (today), and future (forever).

It is important to identify the dimension from which we see, in which we live, and toward which we press. All our mental processing comes from time and place. Therefore, it is easy for our minds, wills, or emotions to be stuck in the past or overwhelmed by the present. Our enemy loves to rule and blind us to the future as God sees it. The enemy knows that when we fear the days ahead or fail to embrace our present reality, we cannot gain the force of vision necessary to maintain our momentum and break forth into "the best" that awaits us from God. He created us to go from strength to strength, faith to faith, and glory to glory. This momentum gives us the energy and strength we need to move beyond our current or past reality.

Therefore, the question is, "How do you see life?" What governs your thought processes and frames the picture of your circumstances? Can you peer deeply into the picture and discern hidden meanings? Can you see beyond the current landscape and into a new faith-framed perspective? Are your carnal mind or emotions controlling the thought processes that interpret what you see, or can you see God working things out to bring about a good end?

How do you see the world around you? How do others see you? How do you perceive that God sees you moving in the earth realm? Your identity shapes how you reflect on and enjoy life. Life involves a process, and we often lose our way amid the events and passing of time, which can create inner conflict. But when you know who you are, inner conflicts decrease. You become confident. Your decision-making is clearer. You display surety. You resist peer and social pressures. You carry an infectious vitality that people seek. Your joy in knowing causes you to be happy. When trials and testing come, you operate in patience and self-control. You make people want to experience the life they witness through you. You appear steady and unwavering. Your mind seems single and settled. You appear whole and at peace. The Lord keeps you in "perfect peace" because your mind is "stayed on" Him (Isa. 26:3).

SEE YOURSELF AS AN ONION WITH LAYERS THAT MAKE YOU CRY. START INSPECTING THE LAYERS ONE BY ONE, FROM THE INSIDE OUT.

See yourself as an onion with layers that make you cry. Start inspecting the layers one by one, from the inside out. If your core is strong, your outward life will reflect your internal strength, with all the fragrance and sweetness of why you were made. Your identity will be intact, and you will be positioned to meet each day with clarity of purpose.

Each day and each person have unique destinies within God's eternal timeline. Each new day strains forward to break the seal and unfurl the next twenty-four hours. This is not only about your overall destiny being fulfilled but about finding its true place and portion within all that God has purposed for each day.

I see each day almost as something sentient and aware of itself, its call, and its purpose in Him. Then, on Shabbat, we stop to look back and project into the future. In our minds we must recover every day that we lose. But in God's time, we can recover a bloodline and generation in a moment. We can redeem the time right amid evil!

Life revolves around seeing ourselves in time and processing our past while walking in the present with a hope and an expectation. Where is the place we are pressing to reach? What will we look like when we get there? To know that we have succeeded and are stronger at the destination than where we started, we must properly balance the time, the place, and our identity as we progress through our days to reach our end.

So how do we develop our identity and wholeness? First, we need to know that we all have an identity and an inheritance attached to who we are. A key to our success in life is how we allow God to develop our inheritance and build us as whole persons. Once we have taken all the parts into account and allowed God to build our whole identity, we understand that within the whole, there is an inheritance—a portion that is for each of us in our life cycle.

The concept of inheritance becomes very important as you advance in understanding your role in the kingdom. Your portion is linked to a promise, and you will need to understand how covenant is established. A *covenant* is an agreement or framework established in the midst of a relationship. When you enter a covenant with God, who can add to you or make you whole, desolation will cease to rule you.

A BLIND SPOT

We all have blind spots that cause us to overlook what we should see or to notice details that aren't truly there. Often our blind spots are metaphorical, involving a lack of self-awareness or sensitivity in a certain area, leading to a prejudice or ignorance about a particular subject. But we can develop physical blind spots too.

I still remember when the eye doctor told me, "You have a blind spot."

I thought, "A blind spot? What could that mean?"

The previous week, my wife Pam and I had attended a Bill Gothard Seminar on Youth Conflicts. The weeklong, well-attended gathering filled the auditorium in Houston. We viewed the service on a large screen at the front of the arena. At the beginning of the week, my eyesight was fine. Yet by the end of the week, I could not see the screen at all. Because I had a demanding job that required constant reading, I assumed I had simply strained my eyes.

Nevertheless, I knew God was doing something major in me. He had already addressed an issue I had been unwilling to face or unable to see in light of His Word. My wife had identified this area and believed I needed Holy Spirit's help trecognize the truth. I guess we all hate having someone point out a spiritual weakness. I certainly did, and I was quick to defend myself. Still, I sensed the Spirit of God revealing truth to me, and I realized the issue from my past needed to be confronted.

But that was only the beginning! When I visited the ophthalmologist on Monday, my life seemed to enter a whirlwind. The test results revealed that a significant portion of my vision was blocked by a small area in my retina that was insensitive to light. The ophthalmologist explained that the problem could involve a tumor on my optic nerve or a blood clot pressing on the nerve and obstructing my vision. Both seemed serious enough that the doctors admitted me to the hospital for further testing. Little did I know, God had planned not just a week of deliverance but a yearlong process—ultimately unfolding into a decade-long journey, resulting in a testimony of freedom.

MAKE MY EYE SINGLE

The Bible says that the eye, the physical organ of sight, is "the lamp of the body" (Matt. 6:22). Biblically, the singleness of one's eye is essential for a person to prosper fully in God's plan, as it causes neither uncertain nor double vision. The eye's integrity matters greatly, because the eye is one of the major gates through which information is received, perceived, and channeled into the human soul and spirit.

It is not surprising that one method of punishment in ancient wars was to blind captives or put out their eyes. (See Judges 16:21; 2 Kings 25:7; Jeremiah 39:7; 1 Samuel 11:2; Zechariah 11:17.) The Bible provides much teaching about the eye. We know that eyes can grow dim with sorrow and tears or waste "away with grief" (Ps. 31:9). Eyes can "run with tears" or "gush with water" (Jer. 9:18). Proverbs 10:10 says that one "who winks with the eye causes trouble," and Proverbs 6:25 warns against those who seduce with their eyes. Psalm 121:1 talks about lifting our eyes to the hills, seeking the help we need to advance in life.

The eye is also used in relationship to the human heart and mind. Ephesians 1:18 (NIV) mentions the eyes of the heart being related to our spiritual perception. With one's spiritual eye opened, the Spirit of God can flow through our lives, and we can receive revelation and enlightenment. Conversely, the Bible warns that we can be spiritually blinded by the enemy's deceptive ways. (See 2 Corinthians 4:4.)

The eye can be good and bountiful or evil and miserly. The eye can be proud, lofty, and haughty, or lowly and humble. According to Job 16:9, we can see rage or anger in a person's eyes. The eye is also used symbolically, being likened to "a fountain of tears" in Jeremiah 9:1, for example. In Proverbs 3:4 and Psalm 101:6, we see sight being related to favor. In Proverbs 6:17 (NIV) we see that eyes can be "haughty." Proverbs 28:22 also speaks of "an evil eye" that lusts after money.[3]

We need to understand the eye as a gate into the soul and spiritual realm of man. The eye is so precious to the human body that God guards us as "the apple of [His] eye" (Ps. 17:8). This metaphor also appears in Zechariah 2:8, which says, "He who touches you touches the apple of His eye."

When your eye is darkened, your whole body becomes dark, and you eventually lose your way. But God's goodness is reflected in a person whose eye is single, meaning it is drawn toward the Lord's purpose and not to the course of this world. James 1:6–8 states this idea somewhat differently, noting that we should "ask in faith, with no doubting, for he who doubts is like a wave of the sea driven and tossed by the wind. For let not that man suppose that he will receive anything from the Lord; he is a double-minded man, unstable in all his ways."

GENERATIONAL INIQUITY IS BLINDING

My family's "good eye" and "evil eye" made for a mixed legacy. Occult practices were not unusual across generations, and I saw them at work. This inherited weakness passed down through my family's bloodline. It was a sinful tendency—an example of iniquity. Such tendencies form patterns that direct us away from God's perfect path.

The root definition of *iniquity* is linked to something "twisted."[4] In other words, you do something that is not equal to God's righteous standard, you resist being reconciled back to God's ways, and your path becomes twisted. Iniquity also weakens your ability to fully embrace God's vision for your life and bring it into full manifestation.

How do iniquitous patterns work? Exodus 20:5 offers the answer: "For I, the LORD your God, am a jealous God, visiting the iniquity of the fathers on the children to the third and fourth generations." Sin affects bloodlines for generations. In Cindy Jacobs's book *The Voice of God*, she explains sin and iniquity in relation to the generations. She points out how the Bible differentiates between sin and iniquity, writing, "Sin is basically the cause, and iniquity includes the effect."[5] Cindy teaches that "a parent can commit a sin such as occultic involvement or sexual sin" and pass it on to the next generation,[6] as children are conceived.

You could say that the sin becomes hidden in the DNA structure of those children and then wars against the divine destiny of the bloodline. I can relate this to the spiritual blind spot I had; it was linked to many inherited occult influences. You may have noticed similar situations in your life, perhaps related to alcoholism, divorce, laziness, or greed—all of which tend to run in families. These are more than learned behaviors; they are manifestations of iniquity that have been passed down. Some patterns are more overt than others.

The occult iniquitous patterns in my family were difficult to detect because of their hiddenness. When I entered the hospital for my physical blind spot, it was as though the Lord had arranged to go deep inside and reveal what had long been hidden. My family was a hardworking, good family with all the potential in the world to prosper. However, the enemy seemed to ravish and destroy all that God had planned. I saw my dad being led astray and involved in gambling, and I saw those who did wicked works of witchcraft.

During my childhood, I understood the supernatural because I watched certain family members operate in those dimensions. My grandfather would speak words and bring change to the elements around him. I would attend "cemetery gatherings," where I heard all sorts of tales—stories of godly, devoted Christians who lived wonderful, spiritual lives and stories of other relatives who reaped disaster.

Some stories were too dark to discuss. Certain cousins would "visit" with a source unknown to me and then watch as the table rose above the floor. At ten years old, I didn't think twice about buying my first Ouija board. No one said it was harmful; it just seemed like any other game. But I also knew that I could ask the board questions, and it seemed to speak back to me.

One side of my family was so steeped in superstition that they kept many wearying rules, and we eventually made mistakes. Other family members were totally devout, praying saints, whose lives reflected a supernatural quality of another kind. Talk about having your eyes unfocused and going in every direction—that was my childhood!

FAMILIAL AND FAMILIAR SPIRITS

Pam had long told me that, at times, something would drive me to react. She could never put her finger on what it was but would say, "It's linked to your family somehow. Every time we almost see what it is, it's like a bat that flies back into the cave. It never comes into the light enough for me to detect it and pull it out of you. But whatever it is, it's very familiar with how certain members of your family operate."

A family, in a traditional sense, can be a group of people living in the same house, such as siblings who share the same parents and bloodline. Through sin and an iniquitous pattern, that bloodline can be affected by a *familial spirit* that controls a certain person or persons in the family. Sin provides an opening for demonic forces to work in subsequent generations, producing iniquity. These forces recognize the family's weaknesses. Therefore, they entice, tempt, or lure family members into the same or related sins.

Familial spirits are assigned to specific families. Some have been in families for generations. They know the bloodline's iniquitous pattern, and they know how it began. They know the iniquity is still active, and they know those to whom it was passed down. Therefore, these spiritual forces or demon entities claim the right to attach themselves to an affected person's soulish nature and hold the bloodline captive to Satan's will.

Familiar spirits work the same way, but they can work outside of a family bloodline. The word *familiar* applies to that which is known through constant association or some sort of intimacy, such as sexual soul ties. The old saying "Birds of a feather flock together" has some validity. The iniquitous pattern in one person is drawn to the same in another. I call this a *cluster of iniquity*. If one member of the cluster dies or refuses the pattern, familiar spirits will seek to reestablish the pattern's strength in the cluster's other members.

DECLARE THAT ALL HIDDEN ISSUES WILL BE REVEALED

I remember attending a certain cell group for prayer. One of the leaders of the group was a spiritual woman who was formerly involved in the occult, especially in studying and practicing under Edgar Cayce. She laid hands on me and declared that anything hidden within me would be exposed.

Oh my, did that stir up a hornet's nest! The enemy wants to

hide himself as he works on diverting us from God's will and blessings. Many of us have a hard time seeing the snare the enemy has planted on our path. Therefore, we step right in it and spend much of our time trying to untangle ourselves. Often, we end up being conformed to the enemy's plot. So instead of staying free to think God's way and walk in the truth of this age, we are molded to the world's ways.

After the woman in the cell group laid hands on me, my blood seemed to curdle. Whatever was hidden at the bottom of my metaphorical "inner lake" floated to the surface, and areas I had been blinded to exposed themselves.

At the time I was trying to finish off projects around our house before heading to the hospital. It was summertime, and my wife's garden (always the most beautiful in the neighborhood) had developed a small brown spot. When she asked me if I could determine its cause, I thought, "Brown spot or blind spot—it all seems like the same process in my life!"

So I began digging around the spot, and the more I dug, the larger the hole became. It was August in Houston—not a pleasant time for yard work, so I became frustrated soon enough. A single brown spot about two inches in diameter had turned into a hole three feet across, and I discovered a major section of concrete that had been hidden underneath our luscious, green yard.

Looking back, this secret was not exposed until the Houston heat reached a certain level. Metaphorically speaking, reactions often occur when pressure rises. The question is how we will respond. When Pam came out to the yard, she suggested a better way of resolving the issue—without ruining the yard for the whole season. As Pam spoke, a strange feeling came over me. I have since remembered what Doris Wagner (wife of the late C. Peter Wagner) always says, "Something 'coming over you' is one way of detecting a demon."

My experience after my wife offered her suggestion was intense: I felt like I was outside my body. I was holding a sledgehammer at the time, and the natural man in me wanted to throw it straight at my wife. Thank God for wisdom, self-control, and a measure of fear: I know my wife, and she, too, can react! So I stopped in the middle of the yard and said, "Lord, I've had this familiar feeling before. Remind me when and how this has happened in the past."

Immediately, the Lord reminded me of when I had what my grandmother called *spells*. Whenever that happened, she would have me lie down and chant certain words until the so-called spell subsided. Now, after Pam's suggestion triggered another "spell," I went inside and lay down on my bed, remembering every word of the chant. But this time I renounced those words, sent them out of my body, and decreed that any power attached to them lost the right to hold me captive. I pleaded the blood of Jesus over myself and my family, and I asked God to fill me anew with the Holy Spirit.

> LITTLE DID WE KNOW, WHEN 2020 ARRIVED, IT WOULD CHANGE THE COURSE OF THE ENTIRE WORLD.

This was a new beginning of true freedom. The hidden issue had eluded detection for decades; but now it came to the surface, and by God's Spirit, I revoked its power to oppress me.

GAINING PERSPECTIVE

Little did we know, when 2020 arrived, it would change the course of the entire world. At Glory of Zion, we start every Gregorian calendar year with a gathering. At Starting the Year Off Right 2020, Cindy Jacobs gave me this word: "I do not see you traveling this year."

I had no idea how the Lord would accomplish this word. Since the 1980s, I have traveled six hundred thousand miles a year, visiting nations across the globe. Then my wife, Pam, said, "The Lord told me at Christmas that you would not be going like you have gone in the past."

Talk about gaining perspective! When you receive words that promise to drastically change your lifestyle, all you can do is watch, wait, and see how God will accomplish what He said. Well, by March 2020, no one was going anywhere, and Charisma House asked if I would write a book about what I was seeing. So I wrote

The Passover Prophecies in the hopes of helping the church understand several key points for the future.[7] I encourage you to read the book if you have not done so already. Meanwhile, here are several insights I made at the time:

- We were entering "a new decade of war—the *pey* decade [in which we would] need to hear God's voice and receive the favor of His hand to discern the critical years ahead."

- "Passover 2020 was prophetically significant, as it propelled the church into a new era for the church—an era [that would require us] to put on the full armor of God (Eph. 6) and remain under the covering of the blood of the Lamb, Yeshua. Positionally in the spirit, we [were to] mark the doorways of our homes—just as the Israelites did on the night of the first Passover—and step into our spheres of influence and authority."

- God was calling us to watch, listen, and move— only according to His direction. We would have to understand how revelation works, realizing that the ensuing war could be won only by knowing God's Spirit and understanding how He communicates through His Word.

- "The first seven years of this *pey* decade (from late 2019 until late 2026) [would] involve critical campaigns in the war, giving the church an unprecedented window to move in fullness for the harvest of millions of souls."

- "In both the physical and spiritual realms, the front line of this war [would] manifest through economic (as well as demonic) power struggles, the realignment of national and geopolitical alliances, and the overall fight for control of world systems (trade, finance, economic influence, power, etc.)."

- The United States was (and is) "equally at a critical crossroads," and the American church was urged to ready itself to let go of the old era. That meant surrendering the past glory and "spoils of former wars" and opening its hand to receive fresh revelation for a new warring season. (I will share later about a dream that God gave me in 2020 predicting America's future.)

- "As we tighten our belts and adjust our spending, the Spirit of God will make us stronger and stronger. As Daniel said, we will learn to do exploits. (See Daniel 11:32.) We will take resources and cause them to multiply in new ways."[8]

Part of gaining a new perspective involves not missing your "new"! When COVID-19 became a pandemic, my worldwide travels indeed ended. In fact, our travels to and from most places in the US proved difficult. Many regulations affected where we could go and what we could do, and masks were required in various establishments. Amid the upheaval, I heard the Lord tell me, "I have determined this time for you. I'm going to do something in you."

I said, "Lord, I don't even know where to start."

The Lord said, "I want you to start in your backyard and work your way out."

The concept of "new" is not always the easiest one to grasp. We hear it a lot—all through the Word of God—and notably in Isaiah 43:19 (ESV): "Behold, I am doing a new thing...do you not perceive it?" Well, we often *don't* perceive it because we don't take time to watch for it. In the past, whenever I'd get back from a trip, I would go to the Israel Prayer Garden, spend time with the Lord, brush off all the "creatures" that had gotten on me during the trip, and get ready to go out again. But this time God said, "I want you to start here in your backyard and work out from there. I am doing a new thing."

So I built fires in our backyard firepit and prayed for people. Praying in the Spirit is important for our spiritual life. I would pray in the Spirit—perhaps three hours each day—knowing I needed a new perspective and asking God for it.

Of course, the Lord knew what my future would require, and He told me to start in my own backyard. I believed that if I obeyed Him, I would gain insight and a new worldview—and it happened! Circumstances began to change, and after several months, I felt ready to go forward again. Suddenly, however, I felt a sharp, knife-like pain in my ear and thought it was the devil. (We always think it's the devil!) I couldn't cope with the pain, and I discovered that I had shingles, in my ear. The doctor wouldn't let me fly, and we had to cancel some meetings.

The Lord said, "I'm still talking to you."

You know, He can get you in enough pain that you'll listen. So I submitted and heard Him say, "Now I can determine your new path." He was ready to give me a new perspective, and I was ready to perceive what He had to show me.

It was worth the wait!

CHAPTER 2

SEEING INTO A NEW DIMENSION

I HAVE WRITTEN SEVERAL books that explain the concept of time, many of which have been published by Charisma House. *Interpreting the Times* gives an account of how time works; *Redeeming the Time* shows how to get your life back on track with a God who loves giving you another opportunity; and *Time to Defeat the Devil* presents strategies for overcoming the enemy's onslaught, deals with trauma, and provides a viewpoint on spiritual opposition.

I have already mentioned *The Passover Prophecies*, and I will be discussing further what I see as our current Passover season. *The Passover Prophecies* offers a proper perspective on the COVID-19 pandemic and discusses how to consider our life ahead. One of my goals in writing the book was to keep us crossing over until we reach a better place.

FROM CRISIS TO RESTORATION

Like everyone I have lived through crises. I have researched both my bloodlines and realized that my identity is not to be bound by them any longer, regardless of how they developed. Nevertheless, the stories remain instructive.

My dad had acquired all the inheritance of his family bloodline. After emigrating from Great Britain and Ireland, the Pierces pioneered and established land in East Texas. The name *Pierce* comes from the same word as *Peter*, meaning "stone, rock."[1] The Pierces were meant to "cut through" and get established in all they did. My dad worked hard to buy each of the twelve sections of land, which had been previously left to his sibling. Yet, despite the potential future before him, life overwhelmed my dad, and he made some bad choices. When he died, I was just sixteen and had to find my way through that great tragedy, loss, and reproach. But God had a plan.

My mother's story was more encouraging. She was a very capable woman from pioneering stock with roots in France. Her people moved to Luxembourg, emigrated to America, and married into the First People of our nation—the Chickasaw. The LeGrands (LeGrone in America) and the Chickasaw produced an incredible, stubborn, and determined bloodline! They came through Nova Scotia and eventually established themselves in East Texas. One international boundary lies within the borders of the United States, and it still exists today. It is land the LeGrones established.

Looking back, God was always there. When I was eleven, I had an experience with His Son, Yeshua. However, trauma, a lack of understanding, and other life situations crowded out that positive experience. My perspective developed around survival and a fight-or-flight way of life. Even then, God was still there, always pursuing me and always ready to step in the exact moment I submitted to Him.

At eighteen years old, I faced a health crisis—a physical collapse that landed me in the hospital and on oxygen. In my hospital room, I saw God's sovereign hand in action as He positioned a Pentecostal pastor in the bed next to mine—a man who introduced me to someone I did not know. Through that experience the Spirit and Word of God became real to me, and my view of life began to change. The Pentecostal pastor encouraged me to spend time in God's Word each day. His exact words were "If you will read a chapter in Proverbs, a chapter in Psalms, a couple of chapters from the Old Testament, and a couple of chapters from the New Testament on a daily basis, you will successfully maneuver through life."

At that juncture, my life began to turn around. Restoration had begun!

YOU HAVE A CORE THAT STABILIZES

How you see yourself from your core determines how you see your surroundings. In the first chapter, I explained some of the core belief systems that form my identity. Each of us has values and interests. We need to know what we believe and what motivates us to accomplish goals in life, because God always causes the best of our core identity to be reflected in the world around us.

Here is what I mean: God tested Abram, and he became Abraham. God moved on Sarai to activate her faith, and she became Sarah. God saw David the shepherd and said, "I've determined that you will be king!" He found an orphan girl, Esther, and made her a queen who saved her people. Jesus met a fisherman named Simon and prophesied that he would be Peter, a rock filled with revelation. Jesus also took a phenomenal but legalistic teacher and revealed grace and power through him—shifting Saul to Paul.

These examples should (1) stir in you a desire to grasp who God meant you to be, and (2) motivate you to do what God means for you to do. I'm talking about the concept of your core—the core that guides and grounds you. The deepest part of your core is what you want to reflect. Be, and become increasingly, a demonstration of your best. Your core sets you apart from others and reinforces your identity. Answers to your difficult decisions arise from your core, which also represents where you belong. How you believe for sustenance or provision, how you believe in your ability, and how you walk and war for freedom derive from your innermost core.

EVER SINCE I MET THAT PENTECOSTAL PASTOR IN MY HOSPITAL ROOM, I HAVE LEARNED THAT THE WORD OF GOD IS LIVING AND POWERFUL.

Here is another way to think of your core. The reactor core of a nuclear plant contains fuel components. There, nuclear reactions take place and heat is generated. The approximate two hundred components that make up the nuclear core generate enough power to affect a region or nation![2] Similarly, your core profoundly affects you and those around you. Therefore, your core and its composition truly matter.

Ever since I met that Pentecostal pastor in my hospital room, I have learned that the Word of God is living and powerful. (See Hebrews 4:12.) Therefore, I have built my inner being by establishing His living Word—the Lord Himself—as my deepest value system. The same power that raised the Son from the grave motivates and moves through my body and out into the atmosphere, wherever I go. To this day I try to demonstrate Him—just as He demonstrated who He was in history. He is as alive today *in me* as He was alive when He walked the earth more than two thousand years ago.

You can see why I believe that the art of meditation and the power of love are the most important principles we can learn. When Joshua entered his new phase of life after Moses's death, the Lord told him how to succeed: It was by meditating in God's Word "day and night" (Josh. 1:8). Why did God say this? Because "faith comes by hearing, and hearing by the word of God" (Rom. 10:17), and because faith works "through love" (Gal. 5:6).

The following are twenty key points that became essential to my understanding. These ideas radically changed me and are now woven throughout my perspective of life. I believe they will add value to yours too!

1. **I had to know the hovering voice of the Spirit.** A voice to speak through chaos always exists. When your voice echoes His own, it creates movement and light that can permeate darkness.

   "In the beginning God (*Elohim*) created [by forming from nothing] the heavens and the earth. The earth was formless and void or a waste and emptiness, and darkness was upon the face of the deep [primeval ocean that covered the unformed earth]. The Spirit of God was moving (hovering, brooding) over the face of the waters. And God said, 'Let there be light'; and there was light" (Gen 1:1–3, AMP).

2. **I had to know how I was made, who I was really like,
and how to exercise the authority I had been given.**
You and I were made in the image and likeness of God,
and He gave us authority.

"Then God said, 'Let Us (Father, Son, Holy Spirit)
make man in Our image, according to Our likeness
[not physical, but a spiritual personality and moral
likeness]; and let them have complete authority over
the fish of the sea, the birds of the air, the cattle, and
over the entire earth, and over everything that creeps
and crawls on the earth'" (Gen. 1:26, AMP).

3. **I had to let the life of Joseph become real to me.**
Like Joseph you have a purpose, and everything you
have been through was for the benefit of others in the
future.

"Now do not be distressed or angry with yourselves
because you sold me here, for God sent me ahead of
you to save life and preserve our family....God sent
me [to Egypt] ahead of you to preserve for you a remnant on the earth, and to keep you alive by a great
escape. So now it was not you who sent me here, but
God" (Gen. 45:5, 7–8, AMP).

4. **I had to know that God heard my cry.** God knows
exactly where you are, and if you seek Him, He will
respond.

"So God heard their groaning and God remembered His covenant with Abraham, Isaac, and Jacob
(Israel). God saw the sons of Israel, and God took
notice [of them] and was concerned about them
[knowing all, understanding all, remembering all]"
(Exod. 2:24–25, AMP).

5. **I had to trust that there is always a way of escape.**
Keep moving forward, and at the right moment, do

what is necessary to reveal the pathway that leads through your situation.

"Then Moses said to the people, 'Do not be afraid! Take your stand [be firm and confident and undismayed] and see the salvation of the LORD which He will accomplish for you today; ... The LORD will fight for you....Tell the sons of Israel to move forward [toward the sea]. As for you, lift up your staff and stretch out your hand over the sea and divide it'" (Exod. 14:13–16, AMP).

6. **I had to learn not to rush but to take ground each day.** Help is on the way. Learn to be patient until you see a full recovery.

"Behold, I am going to send an Angel before you to keep and guard you on the way and to bring you to the place I have prepared....I will send hornets ahead of you which shall drive out the Hivite, the Canaanite, and the Hittite before you. I will not drive them out before you in a single year, so that the land does not become desolate.... I will drive them out before you little by little" (Exod. 23:20, 28–30, AMP).

7. **I had to understand that I could be prosperous if I helped my mind and perspective to develop properly.** Follow this essential command:

"This Book of the Law shall not depart from your mouth, but you shall read [and meditate on] it day and night, so that you may be careful to do [everything] in accordance with all that is written in it; for then you will make your way prosperous, and then you will be successful" (Josh. 1:8, AMP).

8. **I had to develop trust and give the first and best of all I have.** When you give God your first and best, He blesses all the rest. If you seek Him first, you will see

the kingdom in and around you. Give accordingly to unlock those kingdoms!

"Trust in and rely confidently on the LORD with all your heart and do not rely on your own insight or understanding. In all your ways know and acknowledge and recognize Him, and He will make your paths straight and smooth [removing obstacles that block your way]. Do not be wise in your own eyes; fear the LORD [with reverent awe and obedience] and turn [entirely] away from evil. It will be health to your body [your marrow, your nerves, your sinews, your muscles— all your inner parts] and refreshment (physical well-being) to your bones. Honor the LORD with your wealth and with the first fruits of all your crops (income); then your barns will be abundantly filled and your vats will overflow with new wine" (Prov. 3:5–10, AMP). "First and most importantly seek (aim at, strive after) His kingdom and His righteousness [His way of doing and being right—the attitude and character of God], and all these things will be given to you also" (Matt. 6:33, AMP).

9. **I had to realize that I could help anyone whom God brought into my life to become successful.** Part of your God-given purpose is helping others! So when God brings them to you, follow through.

"And all your [spiritual] sons will be disciples [of the LORD], and great will be the well-being of your sons" (Isa. 54:13, AMP).

10. **I had to refuse to shrink back in fear from proving what I believe.** God proves Himself to us continually, and we must faithfully believe Him.

"'You are cursed with a curse, for you are robbing Me…. Bring all the tithes (the tenth) into the storehouse, so that there may be food in My house, and test Me now in this,' says the LORD of hosts, 'if I will not

open for you the windows of heaven and pour out for
you [so great] a blessing until there is no more room
to receive it'" (Mal. 3:9–10, AMP).

11. **I had to grasp how faith and authority work
together.** Just as the centurion understood and recognized authority, you and I must learn about the
authority God has deposited in our lives and understand the authority we are to exercise.

"When Jesus heard this, He was amazed and said to
those who were following Him, 'I tell you truthfully, I
have not found such great faith [as this] with anyone
in Israel'" (Matt. 8:10, AMP).

12. **I had to acknowledge that the Spirit of God still
hovers, and if I listen and meditate, I can understand
the impossible things He can do for me.** Learn not to
try and figure it out; simply ponder what God is doing.

"For with God nothing [is or ever] shall be impossible" (Luke 1:37, AMP). "Mary treasured all these
things, giving careful thought to them and pondering
them in her heart" (Luke 2:19, AMP).

13. **I had to recognize that there is power in connecting
my future to my past season, before I advance.** Jesus
couldn't fulfill His ministry without connecting with
John the Baptist and being baptized by him. There is
always a forerunner who goes before you.

"Then Jesus came from Galilee to John at the Jordan
[River], to be baptized by him. But John tried to prevent Him [vigorously protesting], saying,
'It is I who need to be baptized by You,
and do You come to me?' But Jesus
replied to him, 'Permit it just now; for
this is the fitting way for us to fulfill
all righteousness.' Then John permitted [it and bap-
tized] Him. After Jesus was baptized, He came up

**THERE IS ALWAYS A
FORERUNNER WHO
GOES BEFORE YOU.**

immediately out of the water; and behold, the heavens
were opened, and he (John) saw the Spirit of God
descending as a dove and lighting on Him (Jesus), and
behold, a voice from heaven said, 'This is My beloved
Son, in whom I am well-pleased and delighted!'"
(Matt. 3:13–17, AMP).

14. **I had to learn not to fear but to embrace my wilderness seasons.** It's a matter of being led through your
testing by the Spirit. Then, all your needs can be met.

"Now Jesus, full of [and in perfect communication with] the Holy Spirit, returned from the Jordan
and was led by the Spirit in the wilderness for forty
days, being tempted by the devil. And He ate nothing
during those days, and when they ended, He was
hungry" (Luke 4:1–2, AMP). "The Test was over. The
Devil left. And in his place, angels! Angels came and
took care of Jesus' needs" (Matt. 4:11, MSG).

15. **I had to become aware of the power that is present
in Communion.** When my perspective is not right, I
take Communion. When you make time to commune
with God in this way, your eyes are opened to the real
issues facing you.

"As He reclined at the table with them, He took the
bread and blessed it, and breaking it, He began giving
it to them. Then their eyes were [suddenly] opened [by
God] and they [clearly] recognized Him; and He vanished from their sight" (Luke 24:30–31, AMP).

16. **I had to learn that my heart was important to my
perspective.** How the heart sees and speaks is the real
key to what you believe. If you keep your heart right
before Him, you will see from His perspective.

"Blessed [anticipating God's presence, spiritually
mature] are the pure in heart [those with integrity,
moral courage, and godly character], for they will see

God" (Matt. 5:8, AMP). The apostle Paul warns, "Be angry, and do not sin" or the enemy will gain a foothold in your heart (Eph. 4:26–27).

17. **I had to understand that grace triumphs over law.** The woman caught in adultery had to choose grace. You and I must do the same. The gift of grace produces in us a need to worship the One who gives grace.

"Jesus said to her, 'Woman, where are they? Did no one condemn you?' She answered, 'No one, Lord!' And Jesus said, 'I do not condemn you either. Go. From now on sin no more'" (John 8:10–11, AMP).

> **THE WOMAN CAUGHT IN ADULTERY HAD TO CHOOSE GRACE. YOU AND I MUST DO THE SAME.**

In John 4 Jesus replied to the woman at the well (Photina, as she is known in some traditions), "Woman, believe Me, a time is coming [when God's kingdom comes] when you will worship the Father....The true worshipers will worship the Father in spirit [from the heart, the inner self] and in truth; for the Father seeks such people to be His worshipers. God is spirit [the Source of life, yet invisible to mankind], and those who worship Him must worship in spirit and truth" (John 4:21, 23–24, AMP).

18. **I had to realize that sin was not to reign in my life.** Sin is never supposed to master us. I remember looking up at the Lord and saying, "Is this really true?" He said simply but loudly, "Yes!"—and He will say the same to you.

"Therefore do not let sin reign in your mortal body so that you obey its lusts and passions. Do not go on offering members of your body to sin as instruments of wickedness. But offer yourselves to God [in a decisive act] as those alive [raised] from the dead [to a new life], and your members [all of your abilities—sanctified,

set apart] as instruments of righteousness [yielded] to
God. For sin will no longer be a master over you, since
you are not under Law [as slaves], but under [unmer-
ited] grace [as recipients of God's favor and mercy]"
(Rom. 6:12–14, AMP).

19. **I had to learn that I could redeem my past and open
my future, but wisdom was required.** The passage
below has become my wife's life scripture. She doesn't
fear evil; she just walks and watches carefully. You and
I can do the same.

"Therefore see that you walk carefully [living life
with honor, purpose, and courage; shunning those
who tolerate and enable evil], not as the unwise, but as
wise [sensible, intelligent, discerning people], making
the very most of your time [on earth, recognizing
and taking advantage of each opportunity and using
it with wisdom and diligence], because the days are
[filled with] evil. Therefore do not be foolish and
thoughtless, but understand and firmly grasp what the
will of the Lord is" (Eph. 5:15–17, AMP).

20. **I had to admit that I can always gain a higher perspective.** When you look around, you will always
find room to go higher and gain a better vantage
point. In part this means not allowing religious traditions to stop you from advancing into new spiritual
dimensions.

"Come up here, and I will show you what must take
place after these things" (Rev. 4:1, AMP).

DOING THE ONE THING THAT UNRAVELS EVERYTHING

In our book *One Thing: How to Keep Your Faith in a World of
Chaos*, Pam and I wrote several stories about grasping reality. The
"simple things" in life usually reveal true value. They get to the heart

of situations and create a faith dimension that we can touch. They even have us touch eternity, which is true reality. I think most of us are searching for reality. I also believe there is only one way to find and distinguish between what is helpful or detrimental in the long run, and that is by reaching for the One who created reality.

During Pam's first pregnancy, she had many troubling experiences. We were living in some hard circumstances, and they were trying to overwhelm our lives. In *One Thing,* I shared:

> I had changed our assignment and moved from being on a church staff to serving at a Boys and Girls Home. There were 100 young people who had problems, a staff with problems, and an organization that seemed to have problems. On top of this, our long-awaited promise of bearing a child had become a reality, yet now we were hearing about all these health problems that could happen to the child as she was knit together in Pam's womb. Additionally, there were financial problems. I was in a walk of faith over finances. We had received a notice from the IRS that I owed some money after leaving my secular job, and we had doctor bills, and so on. And on top of this, Pam had lost the use of her left arm during her sickness. I'm telling you—it was a mess!
>
> One night I felt overwhelmed by the world's circumstances. I made a list of everything that was overwhelming me. I looked at the list that had seven major categories and felt totally overwhelmed. I laid the list aside and went ahead and completed the next day's duties and issues. Later that night I could not rest. Therefore, after Pam went to bed, I took my list and went outside in the field and sat before the Lord.
>
> Prayer can take different forms. I knew that the only way I could make it through all these issues was for the Lord to somehow intervene in my life. I held the list up to the Lord and said, "Read this list!" I knew the Lord understood all the issues on the list, but it was like I just needed Him to see what was bombarding me at this point.
>
> I am sure some of you reading this have felt this way. I

I THINK MOST OF US ARE SEARCHING FOR REALITY.

then said to the Lord, "What is it that You would have me do with all of this?" And I sat there. By this time, it was around 11:30 p.m., and I wondered if I was going to sit out in the field all night. A few moments later I felt a very clear impression. I heard that wonderful voice say, "Buy your wife a new dress." Now, I only had $67 in our bank account. But I knew His voice.

This was the Thursday before Easter. I knew I was not working on Friday, so I took my list and wrote at the bottom of it what the Lord had asked me to do.

The next morning I told Pam that we were going to go shopping to buy her a new dress. She questioned me for a moment, but then I said, "It's just what we are supposed to do." We went and bought a new dress, on sale. We then had lunch at a cafeteria and came home. I had two dollars left. Therefore, when the offering plate was passed on Sunday, I just threw those two dollars into the plate and said, "Lord, me and my list are now yours."

It was amazing what happened next. I looked up in the midst of the choir where my wife sang. While the preacher was preaching, I saw someone throw their hand up in the air. It was Pam! This was not a place that you would have thought a person would be having a spiritual experience of overwhelming praise. The message was not that moving. In fact, it was sort of boggy. On the way home after church I said to Pam, "What were you doing throwing your hand up in the midst of that terrible sermon?"... I did not see any reason for praise.

Pam said to me, "During the service I reached down to pull up my pantyhose and the Spirit of God touched me and healed my arm!" THIS WAS ON MY LIST! She continued, "I could do nothing but throw my arm up!"

I countered, "But the message was so awful. The pastor was even sharing how healing was not in the atonement."

She promptly said, "I am sure glad that God didn't listen to his message."

The Lord had read my list and heard my prayer. Within the next six months, EVERYTHING ON THE LIST was

taken care of. All it took was me doing the one thing the
Lord asked me to do: *buy my wife a new dress.*[3]

Let me give you some context for this testimony: Because Pam's
worship had never been extroverted, her exclamation came as a
shock. That day's sermon not only denied healing as part of God's
atoning grace but also claimed that the Lord was not that inter-
ested in our daily provision. The message *totally* contradicted
what I believed and hoped to gain through faith!

God's plans were not hindered by the preacher's words. Instead,
one act of faith changed my whole perspective on how God moves
on our behalf, and it taught me that faith requires action. This
was an important lesson for me, because the reality we see is subject to the reality that can be seen only by faith.

WHAT WE SEE BY FAITH IS REALITY

What we see by faith is reality. Usually, the complicated circumstances around us bind us to the wrong thought process. Belief is
linked with faith, which is linked with glory and reality. In the
Western world, we really don't see God's glory
realm as reality. Our thought processes are
conformed to the visible world around us, and
the trauma we experience becomes embedded
in our souls and understanding.

THE REALITY WE SEE IS SUBJECT TO THE REALITY THAT CAN BE SEEN ONLY BY FAITH.

We can access the realm of reality only
through faith in the One who made us and
has the full picture of what we are becoming.
Faith requires action from us—some sort of response to what we
believe. Let me say it this way: All it takes to experience reality is
one simple faith action, and all the world's complexities begin to
dissipate! Our thinking will either be conformed to the world's
blueprint or transformed by the renewing of the mind, which
allows us to think the way our Creator thinks.

As you seek a clear vision of a new dimension, keep in mind
the twenty points I shared in this chapter. The weaving together

of these ideas reveals my perspective of life—past, present, and future—which I hope clarifies your own way of thinking. Because these ideas strengthened my core, produced a new reality in my life, and enabled me to gain perspective by "looking through" life's many challenges, I believe they can do the same for you.

CHAPTER 3

SEEING FROM YOUR PAST AND INTO THE FUTURE

Time is a kind of circle in which we row backward to enter the future. One of the most difficult concepts for humans to understand is the difference between time and eternity. Everything we do on earth is locked in a timeline. We are living *in* time, but our Creator, who is eternal, is not. We mistakenly see eternity as a measure of time that we equate with *forever* (a really long time, in our minds). But this is also incorrect. Eternity cannot be measured; it exists wholly outside the concept of time. Eternity is every state and every moment.

This brings us to *perspective*. If you stand on a line at Point A and look down that line for Point F, G, or H, you most likely can't see the destination you are striving to reach. The objects around Point A will obscure your view as you look toward Point H, for example. However, if you can rise above the level of the line, you will begin seeing even as far as the horizon. If your viewpoint is high enough, you will see that all the points from A through H are available at one time.

> **TIME IS A KIND OF CIRCLE IN WHICH WE ROW BACKWARD TO ENTER THE FUTURE.**

Time, however, looks more like a circle than a straight line. Remember, we are made in the image of God, who is the same yesterday, today, and forever. Similarly, we have a past, a present, and a future. If we are seeking Him, He can bring our past—even the generational past—into our present and give us the power to overcome challenges that were not conquered in previous generations. Overcoming realizes blessings that your family bloodline has never attained!

This concept is useful when we view it spiritually rather than physically. Remember, God made us in His own image, and God is spirit. Of course, levitating in midair and attempting to see what is ahead and behind us would defy the physical laws of this earth. Doing that would require some kind of flight vehicle. However, if we are saved, we are seated in heavenly places, and our spirits are eternal. Therefore, we can access a realm that is *outside* the timeline in which we live.

In other words, we can access eternity—and what a life-changing realization it is!

We arrive at seasons in life that seem very familiar to us. Yet we must be empowered to recognize moments of decision that can change everything! Recently, Pam and I rewatched the *Back to the Future* three-movie series. I asked Justin Rana, one of the men with whom we work, to watch the series as well. Justin is a highly gifted, tech-savvy person who is human and therefore prone to limiting human thought processes. As we analyzed the *Back to the Future* films together, we enjoyed a riveting conversation. The following section reflects some of our discussions.

BACK TO THE FUTURE TO ACCESS ETERNITY

Have you ever noticed how certain moments seem to repeat themselves? Have you ever thought, "I've seen this before"?

That is how the *Back to the Future* character Marty McFly must have felt. For those of you who have not seen the first *Back to the Future* movie, here's the premise: Marty McFly travels thirty years backward in time from 1985 to 1955 in a somewhat unplanned and accidental way. He travels in a DeLorean time machine, built by Dr. Emmett Brown. To travel in time, the machine must reach exactly 88 mph (an interesting choice of numbers, given that the number eight represents new beginnings in Hebraic thought), and the machine's special flux capacitor must be supercharged with 1.21 gigawatts of power.[1] That's quite a charge!

In his 1985 world, Marty sees his father George McFly as a pushover and fears becoming like his dad. When Marty arrives in 1955, he witnesses his father as a teenager being bullied. Although Marty's primary goal is to return to 1985, the story reveals the redemptive moments in time. Through Marty's visit to 1955, George's timeline changes, and he overcomes his weakness. When Marty returns to 1985, his father is a strong, successful leader whose enemies are under his feet. Marty is pleasantly surprised to see that even George's marriage has improved.

> **MUCH THE WAY MARTY WAS ENABLED TO REDEEM TIME FOR HIS FATHER, THE HELP OF HOLY SPIRIT CAN EMPOWER US FOR HIS REDEMPTIVE PURPOSES.**

I'm certainly not saying that *Back to the Future* is exactly how life works, but there are parallels to be drawn. For example, the supercharged flux capacitor can parallel the born-again person's spirit life. When you submit your spirit to the Father of your spirit, you are filled with Holy Spirit. You live in time, but you are not limited by time. When your spirit is supercharged with the power of Holy Spirit, you can redeem past mistakes, see beyond the present into the future, and access eternity.

This requires having a developed "flux capacitor." We cannot live mundane routines, repeating the same practices day in and day out—not checking in with the Lord, barely praying, and never being "charged" with the Word yet expecting to see beyond our next step on earth. Accessing eternity requires spiritual power. We must submit our faculties to the One who created us, and we must let Holy Spirit activate us beyond ourselves!

Much the way Marty was enabled to redeem time for his father, the help of Holy Spirit can empower us for His redemptive purposes. At one point in *Back to the Future*, Marty and his father discuss his father asking Lorraine (Marty's eventual mother) to the dance. George confesses his fear to Marty, saying, "What if she said no? I don't know if I could take that kind of a rejection."[2] Earlier in the movie (in 1985), Marty talks to his girlfriend about the same kind of fear. As a musician in a band, he's terrified of being rejected by the industry. He tells her, "What if they say I'm no good? What if they say, 'Get out of here, kid. You got no future.' I mean, I just don't think I can take that kind of rejection."[3]

The fear of rejection was passed down from father to son. Marty recognizes the danger of this pattern and works to ensure that George takes steps to overcome his fear. As a result, everything changes for George and for the McFly bloodline.

Generational change does not require a time machine. Through the Spirit of God, we can right wrongs, arrive at critical moments of decision, and see the gravity of the varied paths that are available to us. We can prophesy, and we can redeem bloodlines! By seeing from an eternal perspective, we are freed from the bonds of time. We can access eternity—and that changes everything!

Of course, this kind of change doesn't happen without a fight. From the beginning the enemy has been at odds with mankind, seeking to control and oppress. God made man, placing him within the boundaries of the Garden of Eden. God made covenant with man, calling him to look after, cultivate, and multiply everything there. God saw that it was not good for the man to be alone or desolate.[4] The lone man would not be complete, either in his portion or inheritance. So the Lord took a rib from the man's frame and made woman from it. A new level of prosperity followed for a time.

However, within our portion creatures shrewder than ourselves exist. We must learn to overcome them, so we can continue prospering and bringing our portion to fullness. This conflict is called *warfare*, which can be internal, external, or both. We are warring over our identity and inheritance—our whole identity and our complete portion of everything within our boundaries. Therefore, the apostle John wrote, "I pray that in every way you may succeed and prosper and be in good health [physically], just as [I know] your soul prospers [spiritually]" (3 John 2, AMP).

Two kingdoms are at war: the kingdom of God and the kingdom of Satan. The kingdom of God is within you! Once you know God's will, you war from your prophetic destiny. God's presence in you causes you to triumph. As you operate in the presence of God, God brings into reality everything He has for you. You enter the fulfillment of your inheritance through relational agreement with the Lord, knowing that your future is dependent upon His presence.

Many aspects of the Greek mindset perceived reality less from the concept of linear time, "prioritizing space" and that which is concrete.[5] The events and interactions of your life are encapsulated in a time frame. When you confront negative patterns from your generations' past, you enter a spiritual and relational dynamic with God—but in your time realm. You are no longer controlled by the concrete structure of your cosmos, and you can anticipate God's intervention, breakthrough, and acceleration.

NATURAL, SUPERNATURAL, OR BOTH?

To develop a clear perspective, you must understand time, space, and positioning. Your identity is not confined to or defined by the world in which you live; rather, it is supernatural. You are spirit, soul, and body, and all three are essential to your wholeness. In fact, your truest identity is linked to the invisible world rather than the natural one. That "real you" is what God intended to be displayed openly.

Some of us never tap into our identity in the supernatural. We focus on our physical and emotional states but neglect our spiritual well-being, often out of a desire to be "practical." I would caution against this approach, as it can stem from a longing for acceptance that keeps us conformed to the world's standards. Romans 12:1–2 steers us away from this way of living:

> Therefore I urge you, brothers and sisters, by the mercies of God, to present your bodies [dedicating all of yourselves, set apart] as a living sacrifice, holy and well-pleasing to God, which is your rational (logical, intelligent) act of worship. And do not be conformed to this world [any longer with its superficial values and customs], but be transformed and progressively changed [as you mature spiritually] by the

renewing of your mind [focusing on godly values and ethical attitudes], so that you may prove [for yourselves] what the will of God is, that which is good and acceptable and perfect [in His plan and purpose for you].

—ROMANS 12:1–2, AMP

The world's blueprint encourages conformity and competition through relativism rather than authenticity. True authenticity in the world requires you to be transformed so you can embody the unique design you were created to exhibit. This process involves developing your walk, work, and worth in the earth realm. You also discover your identity in the spiritual realm as the Lord conforms you by the Spirit. You are a gifted, dangerous individual in your enemy's eyes. Therefore, you need to know your strengths, weaknesses, emotions, and talents. Most importantly, you must identify and activate your motivational, ministry, and governing gifts. You never want to attempt to be something you are not. However, you need to remember the divine design: You were created with the capacity for God to live within you, using all you are to reflect in the earth realm the highest qualities possible in your generation.

YOU ARE A GIFTED, DANGEROUS INDIVIDUAL IN YOUR ENEMY'S EYES. THEREFORE, YOU NEED TO KNOW YOUR STRENGTHS, WEAKNESSES, EMOTIONS, AND TALENTS.

God has given you an identity in the spiritual realm, and you confront that realm with each step you take. Demons, powers, and principalities know that you have a destined purpose. Therefore, they must work to hinder, impede, block, and separate you from your best self. To maneuver creatively in overcoming power, your inner core must remain connected, aligned, and empowered by and with the Creator.

This alignment demands a clear image of self. So see yourself in definite terms as a seed planted in time and filled with identity. That identity is expressed through being chosen to produce and grow. Your identity came in seed form; the seed was packed with identity from the beginning. Until that seed comes into fullness, your identity is not fully expressed.

The Hebraic concept of identity is linked to the seed, which is subjected to the supernatural force of being chosen. The principle of being chosen is found throughout the Word of God in relation to identity. For example, the seed of Adam was in both Abel and Cain, but Abel was chosen and favored. The same was true of Jacob and Esau. A certain seed is favored because of its response to the light. May your reaction to light cause you to be chosen—and may you and your seed prosper as you read this book!

THE KINGDOM OF HEAVEN

Throughout the Bible we see the terms *kingdom of heaven* and *kingdom of God*. It is important that we understand and embrace the biblical meanings expressed through these terms. Those who willingly subject themselves to the sovereign rule of a holy God are aligned with kingdom principles. The kingdom of heaven represents the rule that God asserts on the earth during a specific period. This is what links kingdom understanding to time. John the Baptist and Jesus announced that the kingdom was "at hand" (Matt. 3:2; 4:17.) In fact, in Luke 17:21, Jesus said, "The kingdom of God is within you." Therefore, we must move when our King moves!

The kingdom of God represents His rule in the earth realm. The manifested rule of God on the earth is always maturing. The King is moving us from simply going to church to understanding His kingdom within our territory. He is bringing us into a place of dominion, occupation, and ruling with Him in the spheres and places He has assigned us.

THE KINGDOM CANNOT BE CONTROLLED BY CIVIL GOVERNMENT.

Jesus taught extensively on the kingdom, and the kingdom is good news! The kingdom is not based on needs. Jesus said, "The poor you have with you always" (John 12:8). We must have compassion for the poor but not allow their needs to be our only motivating desire in ministry. Jesus commissioned us to work with the poor, orphans, and widows. But He also showed us how to worship Him lavishly as Mary did in John 12:1–3.

The kingdom cannot be controlled by civil government. Through the ages civil government has attempted to govern and rule God's government in the earth. However, the kingdom is not based on worldly systems or patterns. Nor can we comprehend the kingdom with our natural minds; human reasoning is at enmity with God and longs to be conformed to the world around it. However, as we renew our minds, we break free of worldly conformity and start to see kingdom life amid the societal structures that are molding us.

The kingdom cannot be obtained through ambition, and even more exciting—it cannot be postponed. The kingdom is filled with power. Over the past two decades, we have seen a kingdom government emerge, preparing us for the next season of God's work in the earth realm. Kingdom people understand kingdom grace. God has appointed kingdom administrators for every age. We find those gifts listed in Ephesians 4:11–14 and will explore them later. But know this: The kingdom is ruled by grace and love—not by rules, regulations, or laws.

PLANTED IN A TIME, A PLACE, AND THE KINGDOM

We must be aware of our placement in the kingdom. God's people— from the "least" to the "greatest"—are planted in time and place. Paul's account in Athens is a perfect example of a believer's faith working from time and place:

> So Paul, standing in the center of the Areopagus, said: "Men of Athens, I observe [with every turn I make throughout the city] that you are very religious and devout in all respects. Now as I was going along and carefully looking at your objects of worship, I came to an altar with this inscription: 'TO AN UNKNOWN GOD.' Therefore what you already worship as unknown, this I proclaim to you. The God who created the world and everything in it, since He is Lord of heaven and earth, does not dwell in temples made with hands; nor is

He served by human hands, as though He needed anything, because it is He who gives to all [people] life and breath and all things. And He made from one man every nation of mankind to live on the face of the earth, having determined their appointed times and the boundaries of their lands and territories. This was so that they would seek God, if perhaps they might grasp for Him and find Him, though He is not far from each one of us. For in Him we live and move and exist [that is, in Him we actually have our being], as even some of your own poets have said, 'For we also are His children.'"

—Acts 17:22–28, amp

Wherever Paul went, he had a clear sense of his placement—not only in time and place but in God and His kingdom. Paul was conscious of these assignments and keenly aware of God's role in moving him through them.

SEE YOUR PROVISION

Abraham was a rich man, most likely the richest person in his part of the world. He went through a process with God that involved leaving his home and business in Ur of the Chaldees, settling in Haran, reforming his supply line, and watching God work on his behalf. The promise of God included material blessing, land, and blessings to all who would connect with and bless him.

WEALTH AND LUST OFTEN BRING OUT THE WORST IN PEOPLE.

In practical terms relocating to Canaan meant leaving Abraham's family inheritance and moving toward a new boundary. However, making this move positioned him to receive God's best for his life. Nevertheless, much warfare followed his choice to follow God, including conflict within his family. He had to eventually separate from his nephew Lot, who always seemed to choose money over morality. (Wealth and lust often bring out the worst in people.) So when Abraham allowed Lot to choose his preferred portion of land, Lot took the very best. Abraham graciously took what remained and trusted God for his portion.

After Lot's departure, God repeated His promise to Abraham: "All the land which you see I give to you and your descendants forever" (Gen. 13:15). Abraham would possess land, he would have children, and the inhabitants of Canaan would even honor him as a ruler. Meanwhile, Lot happily settled in Sodom and became a victim of war when the region's major kings engaged in violent conflict. (See Genesis 14.)

Regardless of Lot's choices, Abraham did not shirk his family responsibility. He mobilized his disciples and went into battle to rescue Lot, retrieving and returning all the property that had been looted. Yet amid his great victory, Abraham remained humble. Having amassed great spoils of battle, he entered a different level of communion with Melchizedek, who was king of Salem and a priest of the Most High God. Melchizedek then released a different type of blessing on Abraham, saying, "Blessed be Abram of God Most High, possessor of heaven and earth; and blessed be God Most High, who has delivered your enemies into your hand" (Gen. 14:19–20).

A blessing indicates that God is the source of all good. The term *blessing* also denotes a pool or spring.[6] God is like a never-ending spring that provides a constant flow of life to His children. When we bless God, we acknowledge His majesty. Abraham gave a portion of what he had to Melchizedek. From that time forward, God found ways to cut covenant with Abraham and ensure a godly covenant with His people in the earth.

This covenant included the blessing of children. Understanding this was difficult for Abraham, because he and Sarah had long been barren. But Abraham and God began communicating, and Abraham received revelation that developed his faith for the future. Abraham knew that having a child—an eventual inheritor of the promise—was essential to having a real future, which Abraham and Sarah longed to build. God created a world in which they would have dominion, and God's covenant with their bloodline secured that world.

DON'T GROW WEARY IN YOUR TESTING PROCESSES

A person's lifetime consists of many periods of testing and growth. From a covenant perspective, Abraham and Sarah serve as our models. They were tested and made mistakes, yet they had faith. Romans 4:3 says that Abraham's believing "was accounted to him for righteousness." He and Sarah gained God's attention through their trials and faith demonstrations. Both are mentioned in the famous faith chapter of Hebrews 11—a chapter that is still being written from generation to generation. God remembers each time we act by faith and according to His will. As we overcome life's challenges, we develop a lasting testimony for the generations to come.

God promised Abraham that his seed would multiply and rule in the earth realm (Gen. 22:17). However, contention, confusion, competition, and discontent resulted from Abraham and Sarah's attempt to work out this promise. The couple grew weary of waiting for a child, and they attempted to secure the inheritance through Sarah's slave, Hagar. Contention between the women escalated, and Sarah finally said, "Cast out this bondwoman and her son; for the son of this bondwoman shall not be heir with my son, namely with Isaac" (Gen. 21:10).

In trying to expedite the promise by human means, Abraham was forced to give up one son to embrace another. This was a major test in Abraham's life and a difficult one. But there were at least nine more. As you read about all these major trials, remember that (1) the Lord Jesus Christ grafted us into all the blessings that God promised Abraham, and (2) our faith is tested just as Abraham's was. In the following ten tests, Abraham modeled the walk of faith for us:

1. Without knowing where he was heading, Abraham left his family, homeland, and the wealth of Ur to follow God (Gen. 12:4).

2. Abraham experienced hunger during a famine in Canaan (Gen. 12:10).

3. Due to corruption in Egypt, Abraham endured Pharaoh's abduction of Sarah (then known as Sarai) (Gen. 12:10–20).

4. Abraham separated from Lot (Gen. 13). Although Lot had not aligned himself with God's purposes, Abraham rescued him by warring with four kings (Gen. 14).

5. After Abraham and Sarah assumed that she would never give birth, Abraham took Hagar as a concubine (Gen. 16).

6. Abraham obeyed God's commandment of circumcision, which necessitated a painful cutting away, both physically and spiritually (Gen. 17:23–27).

7. Because Abraham tried to protect himself by deceiving Abimelech, Abimelech took Sarah as his wife (Gen. 20:2). Abraham's deception became a pattern in the bloodline of his descendants.

8. When Sarah mistreated the pregnant Hagar, Hagar fled (Gen. 16:5–14). In Genesis 21:8–21, Sarah told Abraham to cast out Hagar and her son, Ishmael, thus forcing Abraham to give up Ishmael.

9. Abraham and Sarah had to believe God's promise of a child despite their advanced age and Sarah's lifelong history of barrenness.

10. The greatest test for Abraham was to trust God with the future and obey His command to give up his son Isaac (Gen. 22:1–14).

TESTING PRODUCES PERCEPTION

Tests produce perception, mold our character, and enlarge us, internally and externally. Testing produces the fulfillment of God's promise and creates a testimony that helps us overcome future crises.

For Abraham his final test was to surrender his future. Losing the hope of someone such as Ishamel to carry on his lineage was painful. But sacrificing Isaac, who represented all hope linked with God's promise for the future, would have been devastating. Yet it was God who told him to take Isaac's life—the same God who had revealed Himself to Abraham, manifested the promise to him, and made covenant with him!

This excruciating test was the faith release that produced Abraham's ultimate testimony and connected prosperity with future generations. Through every test and even Abraham's imperfect responses, he submitted his heart to God and was eventually exalted. The final test displayed his complete trust in the God he followed from Ur of the Chaldees, into Canaan, down to Egypt, into the midst of the Philistines, and then to Mount Moriah.

When the Lord commanded Abraham to offer up his "only son [of promise]," Abraham obeyed (Gen. 22:2). What extraordinary faith! His story shows that with every test, our faith level must rise, and we must choose what to say. When Abraham arrived at the site God selected for the sacrifice, he made a major statement of faith, telling his attendant, "The lad and I will go yonder and worship, and we will come back to you" (v. 5).

That was a faith declaration! Abraham did not know how God's command would ultimately play out. But he did know the God whom he had followed for decades. The *how* was not the issue. (It never really is.) The significant key to Abraham's future was in knowing God and trusting Him. So when the Lord called out to him, Abraham said, without hesitation, "Here I am" (v. 1).

It is widely thought that when Abraham and Isaac traveled to Mount Moriah, Abraham was almost 140 years old, and Isaac was perhaps thirty-six or thirty-seven years old. The aged Abraham could not have forced his adult son to accept this test. Yet, in

Genesis 22, we see the two men moving in complete harmony. When Isaac realized that he was the offering, he asked his father, "Where is the lamb for the burnt offering?" (v. 7).

Abraham replied by faith in verse 8. If I might paraphrase, he said, "God Himself will seek out and provide the lamb. His plan of provision is great, and we will see it manifest! But if there is no lamb, then you, my son, will be the offering."

Imagine saying that to your beloved son! But Abraham was determined to remain faithful to God. Therefore, he passed this very difficult test and received perception: He saw the ram God provided, and Isaac's life was spared.

REJOICING TO OBEY; NOT SO HAPPY IN THE PROCESS

There is a joy in fulfilling God's will. Feelings follow faith, but like Abraham we sometimes feel sad about choices that leave our future hanging in the balance. Binding Isaac on the altar represented total submission and the laying down of potential future generations. However, faith and obedience then revealed what had been hidden from view: When Abraham lifted his eyes, he saw God's provision, and in an instant his vision for the future opened.

We know that God spoke again and included the generations in His next promise. However, Abraham and Isaac had to believe all that by faith. The perfect outcome required Isaac to submit, which he did. He trusted his dad and, like his dad, he had to trust that a sacrifice would appear in time for his life to be spared. As father and son submitted themselves, the promise for their shared future was extended to the seed of generations to come.

> The Angel of the LORD called to Abraham from heaven a second time and said, "By Myself (on the basis of Who I Am) I have sworn [an oath], declares the LORD, that since you have done this thing and have not withheld [from Me] your son, your only son [of promise], indeed I will greatly bless you, and I will greatly multiply your descendants like the stars of the heavens and like the sand on the seashore;

and your seed shall possess the gate of their enemies [as con-
querors]. Through your seed all the nations of the earth shall
be blessed, because you have heard and obeyed My voice."

—GENESIS 22:15–18, AMP

When we move in obedience, our "seed" becomes able to repro-
duce prosperity and promise. God proved this in Abraham's life,
and He proves it when we submit in our seasons of testing. As we
choose to obey, the provision for our future awaits us—and not
only provision but also the revelation that releases vision.

In Genesis 22:14 Abraham named the place where the ram was
revealed; he called it Jehovah Jireh, meaning "the Lord will provide." God was not only the One who provided but the One who
caused Abraham to see his provision. This event became a prototype of genuine faith. Ever since, any descendant of Abraham—
whether naturally descended or grafted in—could obey God and
see both their provision and the future God has promised.

REFLECTING A NEW, TRANSFORMED IDENTITY

The mind is dynamically intertwined with the heart and spirit.
Therefore, we need to investigate the workings of the mind in relation to the whole person. I recently wrote the following note to
someone close to me who was experiencing a terrible ordeal and
questioning the future for themselves and their loved one:

> The mind can dream beyond the boundaries of the present
> reality that confronts it on a daily basis. Whatever the mind
> can conceive, believe, and achieve is the key to the future,
> no matter which circumstances or obstacles may be sur-
> rounding the situation. The pure in heart see God. As we
> purify our thoughts from past traumas and limitations, we
> begin to see our present reality as God sees it. With God, all
> things are possible. With our finite thinking, we limit His
> possibilities in the situation confronting us.
>
> Quiet your emotions and see all your present blessings....

Look beyond your past traumas, failures, shortcomings, and hurts, and see the deepest desires that each of you have for the future. Redevelop honesty, honor, and trust toward Him and each other. Let the Lord reveal how you can lay down your right of way and attain the best that is waiting for you. Only He can accomplish this, by His Spirit in each of us.

The Hebrew mind did not think of the passage of time quite like the ancient Greek mind did. The view of time in our Western civilization is more closely aligned with the Greeks. Hebrews identified the passage of time in terms of the *life cycle*. They saw man as participating in two dimensions of time. One "age" of time was temporal: We were placed within the natural realm and lived according to its rhythms and the laws of science. The other dimension of time was an age to come:

> We speak wisdom among those who are mature, yet not the wisdom of this age, nor of the rulers of this age, who are coming to nothing. But we speak the wisdom of God in a mystery, the hidden wisdom which God ordained before the ages for our glory, which none of the rulers of this age knew; for had they known, they would not have crucified the Lord of glory.
>
> —1 CORINTHIANS 2:6–8

The wisdom that God has reserved for the current moment is available to us. We can gain wisdom that no enemy from hell can access. In the Hebraic mindset, events that occur throughout life create smaller temporal cycles, which reflect life's bigger picture. Summing up these smaller cycles determines the finite age but without limiting us to the events of this age. The sum of all the temporal events in an age produces a finite cycle of life, but the sum of events in the age to come is infinite, which means it is *everlasting*.

In the ancient Hebrew culture, life was defined by events connected to relationships. In our culture we like to *feel time* and are constantly worried about having *enough time*. To the Hebrew mind, time was not an object; therefore, they could not lose time, but they could lose relationship. As a result, they could fail to *sum up* the events that would otherwise comprise their finite lives.

This Hebraic way of thinking has profound effects: If you think from a relational perspective, you regain the sense that you are important and that you are placed on the earth to accomplish a full purpose. You live your best life when you stay in relationship, define events around relationship, and fully accomplish all that the relationship requires.

In other words, your true identity is linked to the highest relationship in your life. If you don't recognize this truth, you will quit choosing *whom* to serve each day. The truth is that your days (and mine) are filled with questions of *how* and *what*—or *whom*—you will serve. This is typified in the juxtaposition between Martha and Mary in Luke 10:38–42: Mary sat at Jesus' feet and developed a relationship with Him, while Martha was visibly distracted by all that needed to be done. Mary embraced the moment, but Martha occupied herself with activity.

We are called to live carefully, "redeeming the time, because the days are evil" (Eph. 5:16). When we become mature in who God intends us to be, we develop the confidence to redeem our mistakes. This clear sense of identity makes us unafraid of the future and prepares us to face death with assurance and a mentality of victory. There are times in our life cycle when the cycle stops and we recognize death, which is like a sting. How we react to the sting determines whether our life cycle continues into its fullness.

The real question when confronting death is whether we (1) withstand the sting, keep standing, and overcome, or (2) become weakened and lose our ability to resist death's attempt to rule and reign in our lives. The entrance of death into our life cycle creates a seed, much like the one referenced in John 12:24, which bears fruit once it dies. To keep standing is to find, cultivate, and produce a harvest from what death meant to take from us. Death intends to hold the seed captive in the ground. But we can take that seed, plant it, and watch our identity grow, multiply, and produce fruit for the future.

I pray that as you become increasingly skilled at seeing from your past and into your future, you will develop a powerful resistance to the awful stings that may have darkened past seasons of your life. Instead, may events in the past create new strength and produce abundant joy. I pray the seeds sown when you died to your last season of life will multiply, create an amazing life, and cause the enemy to be fully overcome. Remember, "unless a grain of wheat falls into the ground and dies, it remains alone; but if it dies, it produces much grain" (John 12:24).

CHAPTER 4

THE POWER OF REVELATION MAKES US A RADICAL PEOPLE

WE ARE A radical people. By embracing the Lord Jesus Christ as the Messiah of a heavenly kingdom beyond any earthly kingdom, we become forceful beings who are dangerous to worldly and demonic systems. Notice how the psalmist spoke to this truth:

> Out of the mouth of babes and nursing infants You have ordained strength, because of Your enemies, that You may silence the enemy and the avenger.
>
> When I consider Your heavens, the work of Your fingers, the moon and the stars, which You have ordained, what is man that You are mindful of him, and the son of man that You visit him? For You have made him a little lower than the angels, and You have crowned him with glory and honor.
>
> You have made him to have dominion over the works of Your hands; You have put all things under his feet, all sheep and oxen—even the beasts of the field, the birds of the air, and the fish of the sea that pass through the paths of the seas. O LORD, our Lord, how excellent is Your name in all the earth!
>
> —PSALM 8:2–9

We must always remember who God is and who He made us to be. We also need to think the way God intended us to think. Remember, developing the core of your being, and revolving that core around the Father of your spirit, allows you to maneuver and triumph in the world around you. Your focus on Him is essential! As Hebrews 12:9 says, "We have had human fathers who corrected us, and we paid them respect. Shall we not much more readily be in subjection to the Father of spirits and live?"

The Word of God reveals three partners in the creation of every human being: The mother who provides an egg, the father who contributes a sperm, and the Almighty who imparts a spirit, which He knits together within every human being. The child who is produced when a mother and father procreate must realign with the One who makes each of us whole. Unless this happens, the person's spirit becomes vexed, and their soul becomes infected.

Human thinking is fundamental to our lives, both physically and spiritually. Two types of human thinking are prevalent: One deals with concepts, while the other processes situations. *Conceptual* thinking is linked with the "act of reasoning," whereas *situational* thinking is linked with our "inner experience."[1] Conceptual thinking aims to increase and enhance knowledge about the world. Situational thinking drives us to understand "our very existence" amid life's circumstances.[2]

Our way of thinking can keep us attuned to where we are and how we are to live. For example, we sometimes talk about the weather as though we are oblivious to our nuclear age and our role in it. This happens when we don't recognize the times. We tend to ignore the problems that seem irrelevant to our individual lives. However, in our rapidly changing world, situations—even those that seem not to involve us—affect us and can provoke and increase our creativity. Through revelation from God and creative strategies, we can overthrow the enemy's plans!

BELIEF AND REVELATION

What we believe is crucial. I absolutely need to believe in someone much greater than myself; we all do! The real challenge involves how we embrace faith and what, or whom, we choose as the object of our faith.

Are our lives centered on the God Most High or on something or someone else? Either way, an act of believing is involved. From our act of believing, we develop the framework of what and how we believe. From there we develop the voice of what we believe. We must constantly remind ourselves what we stand for and then align ourselves with it. These choices need to be clear to us and others. In other words, we need to examine ourselves at the level of our chosen belief system.

Revelation is the uncovering of something not previously disclosed. Suddenly, you just *know*. During a problem, the answer pops into your mind. Then you consider what God expects you to do with that answer. This thought process causes you to rely not on yourself, or your talents, abilities, and emotional insights, but on what God reveals and requires.

GOD'S PERFECT PLAN AWAITS DISCLOSURE

We must remember that, when Satan fell, he used his character—his gifts, personality, and inclinations—to accomplish on earth what God had created him to accomplish in heaven. Ezekiel 28:14–15 says, "You were the anointed cherub who covers; I established you; you were on the holy mountain of God; you walked back and forth in the midst of fiery stones. You were perfect in your ways from the day you were created, till iniquity was found in you."

When Satan was cast down, his role became to cover over every structure that would prosper humankind in the future. Because of his fall from God's grace, Satan's redemptive purpose was infected by iniquity. Therefore, everything he touched in the earth realm became contaminated. The only place of safety from this disease was to return to God's original plan of redemption for us.

From the Garden of Eden until today, Satan has sought to undermine revelation and God's perfect plan by provoking fear with a question: "Did God really say" that? (Gen. 3:1). Satan wants us to believe that God is withholding something—that He is unwilling to reveal His heart for our prosperity. The moment we buy into this idea, we embrace Satan's iniquitous plan, which only obscures our path.

Many people believe that God has inflicted evil upon us. They demand to know how almighty God could allow the enemy to work in the earth realm. But we must remember that everything God created was meant for a higher purpose. Therefore, anything that seems bad may actually be a redemptive blessing waiting to be uncovered. If we understand that God is good and created us to experience all His goodness, we will strive to uncover the good plan that is hidden in every invasive incident, trial, and trauma that comes our way.

THINK OF YOURSELF AS A FLOWER: WITHOUT THE SUN—THE SOURCE OF ENERGY THAT PROPELS GROWTH AND CAUSES YOU TO BLOSSOM— YOU CANNOT GROW.

How you allow life's difficulties to work on your behalf becomes a key to your success. Revelation is the only way to uncover a more excellent way to walk. Think of yourself as a flower: Without the sun—the source of energy that propels growth and causes you to blossom—you cannot grow. You must learn to interact with your Maker, just as the flower interacts with the sun. In fact, the sun warms the soil, helping the seed to germinate in hopes of creating an incredible blossom.

Revelation works in much the same way. The only real question is whether the seed will respond to the revelation and align itself with God's thoughts. As Isaiah 55:8 says, "'My thoughts are not your thoughts, nor are your ways My ways,' says the LORD." Revelation realigns us with God's perspective. When your ideas are aligned with the way God thinks, prosperity and fulfillment can follow.

YOU HAVE ACCESS TO REVELATION

Revelation (or the lack thereof) ultimately determines the quality of our lives. We tend to forget who we are. That is probably why I love the Christmas season and Christmas movies so much: They remind us that Jesus came to the earth to redeem us. If we don't celebrate that truth, we forget who we are and why we are here.

One of my favorite holiday stories is Charles Dickens's *A Christmas Carol*. In the tale Dickens explores a man's life in terms of past, present, and future, showing us how easily we can miss opportunities in our lives. We need to understand that the Lord never intended for us to miss opportunities. Yet, because of the choices we make, we sometimes do. That is exactly what happened to Ebenezer Scrooge, who missed countless opportunities to enjoy and appreciate life. In another Christmas classic *It's a Wonderful Life*, the present came crashing down on a man named George Bailey and almost left him without a present, past, or future. Bailey became so despondent that he wished he had never been born. In the end both these characters stopped to consider and celebrate the miracles they once overlooked. This brought the redemptive purposes from their past into the present, and the future opened before them.

In films and in life, there is always an antagonist or an issue we must face to overcome a difficulty. Therefore, we need to actively remember why Jesus came. He said, "The thief does not come except to steal, and to kill, and to destroy. I have come that they may have life, and that they may have it more abundantly" (John 10:10). We need to take these words of Jesus to heart and ask ourselves, "How has the devil robbed me from enjoying life in abundance?"

This question will help you acknowledge any areas in which God's promised fullness to overflowing is lacking. It will also help you identify your enemy, pinpoint what he is trying to accomplish in your life, and adjust your outlook for the better. Remember that, by the Spirit, you have access to revelation, which shapes your perspective and causes you to see. So let God reveal and remind you of who you are, who He is, and what He has promised.

KNOW THE ENEMY OF YOUR FULLNESS

It's time for me to present the enemy in a way I have never presented him before. It is imperative to recognize him and his work, because until you do, you can only wonder why certain situations happen. I can remember being a young man, looking back on my life and seeing the devil's handiwork. I realized that he had decimated our family and was determined to steal our inheritance. I knew I had to align myself with someone greater than him and all he had done. But how would I do that?

I was just eighteen years old. I had been going to church and had even experienced salvation. But then God suddenly became real to me. The Lord somehow opened my eyes and revealed all the enemy's toeholds in my heart. I said, "Lord, how am I going to kick him out?"

I heard the Spirit of God speak to me from 1 John 4:4 (KJV): "Greater is he that is in you, than he that is in the world."

> I WAS JUST EIGHTEEN YEARS OLD. I HAD BEEN GOING TO CHURCH AND HAD EVEN EXPERIENCED SALVATION. BUT THEN GOD SUDDENLY BECAME REAL TO ME. THE LORD SOMEHOW OPENED MY EYES AND REVEALED ALL THE ENEMY'S TOEHOLDS IN MY HEART.

Deep down I knew it was true. We all know the truth, but we don't always understand how to get back what has been stolen or destroyed by our poor choices. We wonder, "How in the world can our regrets from the past be redeemed?"

You already know what happened the week after I was arrested by 1 John 4:4: I collapsed, was hospitalized, and was on oxygen for two weeks. God put me in a room with a Pentecostal preacher who introduced me to Holy Spirit, who overwhelmed me for three days and transformed my life.

After that encounter, three distinct passages became real to me—weapons I would use for the rest of my life. Of course, God's Word itself is a weapon that empowers us to withstand any onslaught. Let's focus on the three passages I believe the Lord gave me all those years ago.

Embracing firstfruits

The first weapon was a passage from the Book of Proverbs:

> Do not be wise in your own eyes; fear the LORD [with reverent awe and obedience] and turn [entirely] away from evil. It will be health to your body [your marrow, your nerves, your sinews, your muscles—all your inner parts] and refreshment (physical well-being) to your bones. Honor the LORD with your wealth and with the first fruits of all your crops (income); then your barns will be abundantly filled, and your vats will overflow with new wine.
>
> — PROVERBS 3:7–10, AMP

Holy Spirit visited me in that hospital, and in that moment God's Word suddenly came alive! I'm glad I embraced that moment, because blessings overwhelmed me—and missing that moment would have meant missing out on the overflow God had planned for me. Obviously, healing was part of God's plan, and if the Proverbs 3 passage is not about healing, I don't know what is. As I read the passage in my hospital bed, I knew God could heal everything in me. Honoring God with my wealth also became real, and I embraced the giving of firstfruits. It wasn't about understanding firstfruits; it was about *embracing* what God said.

God said, "Here is your first weapon. If you take and use it from this day forward, you will experience a total reversal of what the enemy has done." That was part of how the Lord uprooted the devil's toeholds from my heart. The revelation needed to dive so deep within me that no devil or crisis could pull it out. That word—that weapon—had to be so well-developed in me that it became more than theological; it became flesh in me and shaped me accordingly.

In the crises to come, I had to learn to access the weapon and use it—and I have done this day after day, throughout the years.

Dealing with emotions

The second weapon was a passage from Paul's epistle to the church at Ephesus:

> BE ANGRY [at sin—at immorality, at injustice, at ungodly behavior], YET DO NOT SIN; do not let your anger [cause you shame, nor allow it to] last until the sun goes down. And do not give the devil an opportunity [to lead you into sin by holding a grudge, or nurturing anger, or harboring resentment, or cultivating bitterness]. The thief [who has become a believer] must no longer steal, but instead he must work hard [making an honest living], producing that which is good with his own hands, so that he will have something to share with those in need.
>
> — EPHESIANS 4:26–28, AMP

Remember, you are human, and anger can grip you. But you don't have to allow it to control and weaken you. For example, don't allow anger to cause you shame, and don't let it last until the sun goes down.

This passage became my second weapon, in part, because it freed me to express my emotions safely, within an appropriate time frame, and without getting into trouble. I learned that if I didn't process my emotions during that period and corral them within the boundaries God established, I would give the devil an opportunity to establish a new toehold in my heart.

The passage from Ephesians 4 shows that capturing your emotions and refusing to repeat the missteps that led you to violate or miss opportunities in the past can transform potentially negative situations into something beneficial: You now have something to share with others in need. So obey the Lord's instructions, and He will deal with any existing toeholds, one by one.

Stripping sin's dominion

The third weapon the Lord gave me was Romans 6:14 (AMP), which says, "Sin will no longer be a master over you, since you are not under Law [as slaves], but under [unmerited] grace [as recipients of God's favor and mercy]."

I asked the Lord, "Is that true?"

He answered, His voice amplified in my hospital room: "Yes!"

However, there was a process: I had to undergo a change to my identity. Sin was not to rule me in ways that caused me to (1) lose favor, (2) forget what God meant to me, or (3) forget who He intended me to be.

Romans 6:14 is a weapon that defined what I was up against and how sin was operating against me. Every time I was tempted to move beyond a boundary the Lord had set for me, I could use that weapon. When I first became acquainted with the verse, I was unable to resist sin in my own strength. I had to allow the One I met under the oxygen tent to rise within me, help me overcome, and keep me from becoming enslaved again.

John's first epistle describes the process I was undergoing: It was the identity change that occurs when we follow Christ in earnest:

> The one who practices sin [separating himself from God, and offending Him by acts of disobedience, indifference, or rebellion] is of the devil [and takes his inner character and moral values from him, not God]; for the devil has sinned and violated God's law from the beginning. The Son of God appeared for this purpose, to destroy the works of the devil. No one who is born of God [deliberately, knowingly, and habitually] practices sin, because God's seed [His principle of life, the essence of His righteous character] remains [permanently] in him [who is born again—who is reborn from above—spiritually transformed, renewed, and set apart for His purpose]; and he [who is born again] cannot habitually [live a life characterized by] sin, because he is born of God and longs to please Him.
> —1 John 3:8–9, amp

I didn't want sin to master me. I didn't want to represent the devil in the earth realm or derive my inner character and values from him. Many people and even nations are embracing the devil's ways. But I knew God wanted me to continue in my new identity—celebrating the Son of God who came to destroy the works of the devil (including those he wanted to accomplish in and through me) and to give me access to a relationship with God.

To understand sin correctly is to realize that it causes you to miss your mark. God is aiming you at a mark—a purpose and destiny for the future. Sin is anything that causes you to deviate from the path of fullness and your mark. Yes, God says, "Do not be drunk with wine" (Eph. 5:18), but He doesn't say, "Don't drink wine." You must know what the mark is and understand what causes you to miss it. You must realize an enemy exists who will use every available resource to get you off track.

You must also know that Yeshua came as the Son of Man to destroy the works of the enemy. "God so loved the world that He gave His only begotten Son, that whoever believes in Him should not perish but have everlasting life" and accomplish all that they have been put on earth to accomplish (John 3:16)!

YOU ARE A WEAPON

The Lord has called you and will develop you as a weapon to destroy the works of the enemy. When the Word becomes flesh in you, your mind will be transformed—rather than conformed to the world's ways—because the living Word came to overcome the world. Wherever you walk, whatever you do, however you move and have your being, you will become a weapon to destroy the devil's schemes!

Whatever boundaries God gives you—whatever space, domain, or work He assigns you—the following keys will help you establish those boundaries:

1. Purpose

2. Access

3. Work (watching, worship, and multiplying)

4. Giving

5. Identity

6. Resourcefulness

7. Empowerment

We will discuss these keys in the following sections, starting with *purpose* and the knowledge that you have a purpose. You were placed on earth so your spirit man could come alive by realigning with the Father of your spirit. You were created to be used as a weapon to defeat the enemy during your life on earth. Your purpose should affect what comes out of your mouth and touch every place you walk—whether you are in prison or free to travel the world.

You also need to know that you have been given *access*. In Genesis 1 God planted a garden and gave Adam access to it. Then God essentially said, "I'm going to trust you to keep access with Me." So Adam was given access to the garden *and* the garden's Creator.

As for *work* God defined Adam's work as watching after the boundaries He gave him, which involved caring for both the space and the responsibilities God assigned. The English word *work* can be used as a verb, noun, or adjective. The Hebrew word is *avodah*, which speaks of worship or work.[3] So worship and work are related. Worship, work, and access are also interrelated: When you keep gaining access to God, you cultivate and multiply everything in your territory. If you maintain your access within the boundaries that you have been given—whether it's a marketplace job, a hospital position, or any other environment—you will move in the life-giving power that brings overflow and may end up ruling the entire space.

The devil's goal is to separate you from access to the One who can cause you to overcome. He wants to discredit who God is within your boundaries. When you agree with the devil, you start losing the access and authority you have been given within those boundaries. This is what happened to Adam. Yet he knew enough about the serpent to name the enemy. He understood the serpent's capabilities and subtlety. Adam also knew that God had established one limitation within the garden: a certain fruit, the eating of which would create death.

So how did Satan entice the man who knew better? He had to convince him that God was not protecting him but withholding from him the best fruit the garden had to offer. Once Adam and Eve accepted the enemy's premise, they lost the access and authority they had enjoyed, and they forfeited access to the fullness of God's intended blessings.

That is what happens when we agree with Satan; we lose access, we lose blessings, and we miss out on God's original intent for us. However, God always has a promise and a restorative plan. In Genesis 3 He essentially said, "I will deal with the enemy. He might win this battle, but he will not win the war!"

Let this truth sink deeply into your core: God has a plan to deal with the enemy! He sent the second Adam, His Son, to destroy the enemy's works. He has granted you access to come into agreement with His Son. The Son, in turn, gives you access to Father's throne room, which is filled with revelation and wisdom to destroy the works of the enemy. Paul expressed the following hope:

> That your faith should not be in the wisdom of men but in the power of God....But we speak the wisdom of God in a mystery, the hidden wisdom which God ordained before the ages for our glory, which none of the rulers of this age knew; for had they known, they would not have crucified the Lord of glory.
>
> —1 CORINTHIANS 2:5, 7–8

Paul went on to explain that God gives revelation to those who love Him. This revelation brings clear perception, enabling us to see all that God has given us.

> God has unveiled them {the things He prepared for those who love Him} and revealed them to us through the [Holy] Spirit; for the Spirit searches all things [diligently], even [sounding and measuring] the [profound] depths of God [the divine counsels and things far beyond human understanding]. For what person knows the thoughts and motives of a man except the man's spirit within him? So also no one

knows the thoughts of God except the Spirit of God. Now
we have received, not the spirit of the world, but the [Holy]
Spirit who is from God, so that we may know and understand the [wonderful] things freely given to us by God.

—1 Corinthians 2:10–12, amp

God will never be your enemy. He is always good and perfect.
He wants all good things to come to you, and He wants to show
you the most excellent path for your life. God longs to reveal
Himself to you, and He wants you to flourish like a flower. God
did not curse humankind—He cursed the serpent and informed
Adam and Eve of some difficulties they would face after the fall.
For example, the woman would have to deal with her desire for
her husband, and the man would have to toil to eat what the
ground produced. (See Genesis 3:16–17.)

What happened in the garden shows that our desire for what we
are not supposed to have leads to loss of access, which negatively
affects our work as a result. As long as man had
access to God, the ground they were given pros-
pered. Once access was lost, the ground resisted
God's original plan, and man had to struggle
with the ground to eat.

GOD WILL NEVER BE YOUR ENEMY.

GENERATIONAL INIQUITY AND THE IMPORTANCE OF GIVING

Generational iniquity may affect future generations, as the consequences of one man's sin can carry forward. Genesis chapter 4
shows that we are held responsible not only for our own sin but
also for patterns of sin in our bloodline before us.

Take Cain and Abel. These two sons of Adam and Eve were
responsible for their work: "Abel was a keeper of sheep, but Cain
was a tiller of the ground" (v. 2). Each man had to manage his
area of responsibility, and each was called to prosper. They had
no access to the garden because the fall occurred before they were

born. Adam and Eve's sin prevented the whole family from seeing the garden continually filled with glory. (See Genesis 3:17–19.)

Yet God gave this first family new ground. Because of the fall, however, the ground was cursed, and bringing it under dominion now required much toil. With the portal—or access—to the presence that Adam and Eve enjoyed in the garden lost, Cain and Abel had to gain access in a new way. But remember—and confess for your own life—that God can give you access anywhere: "The earth is the Lord's, and the fulness thereof" (Ps. 24:1, kjv). Therefore, you have access no matter where you are.

So in Genesis 4:4, we find Abel busy raising livestock, while his brother Cain tilled the ground. When the time came to give their firstfruits, "Abel…brought of the firstborn of his flock and of their fat," which satisfied God's heart. Because "the Lord respected Abel and his offering," he had access to God.

Cain had a different approach to his firstfruits: He brought whatever he wanted to bring. Therefore, God "did not respect Cain and his offering" (v. 5), and Cain became angry with his brother as a result. God addressed Cain's resentment and essentially said, "You can have access too, if you want to give me the best that you have. But Cain if you don't, sin is going to be at your door; iniquity will come to the door of your future." (See Genesis 4:7.)

Cain grew so angry that he killed Abel, and Abel's blood seeped into the ground. (See Genesis 4:8, 10.) The ground suddenly took on a new, awful identity. Cain lost access fully and was destined to wander the remainder of his life. This altered his identity, which is the real goal of all iniquity: You lose your way and never find the best that God has prepared for you.

Giving is vital as you war against the devil's attempts to strip away God's intended identity from you. You must contend with the consequences of the devil's iniquitous plan. Remember, Yeshua came to destroy the works of the devil and fully restore our access—wherever we are and whatever the time.

In John 8:44 Jesus described the devil as the father of lies:

> You are of your father the devil, and the desires of your father you want to do. He was a murderer from the beginning, and does not stand in the truth, because there is no truth in him. When he speaks a lie, he speaks from his own resources, for he is a liar and the father of it.

The devil can't do anything except speak to and manipulate a toehold within you that aligns with his nature like unforgiveness, hatred, lying, or deceit—a "resource" that allows darkness to operate in our lives. Before Yeshua ascended, He told His disciples He would leave Holy Spirit on earth. If you allow Holy Spirit to come into and empower you, He will push all the enemy's resources out of you, leaving nothing more for the devil to influence. The enemy will have no choice but to surrender his access.

Through Holy Spirit and faith in Yeshua, we have constant access to the Father. This access is what God offered us from the beginning, and it became available when the Son arrived. The Father offered humankind full access to all His riches again. The Son gained access to mankind and presented the Father's heart. He gave us the ability and authority to uncover and destroy every work of the enemy in the earth realm.

Too often, however, the trials of life cause us to lose sight of this fact. Have you allowed past hardships to preoccupy you? Are they causing you to hate the present moment and miss God's best along the way? If this continues, you will eventually lose sight of the future and be reduced to wandering, as Cain was. Your outcome is largely tied to how you handle your emotions. Every time you let your emotions take you outside the boundary within which God intended you to rule, you lose access.

Tell the Lord today, "Lord, I want to keep access to heaven. I want to give You access to me. I want that access to multiply. I want to overflow everywhere I go. I want to enjoy life. I want to recognize when my enjoyment of life is being taken from me. I want to war against the one who is robbing me!"

You can gain access to God wherever you are—even on death row. Really, we are all on death row until we embrace the life, revelation, and wisdom that God offers us. So here is my prayer for you and anyone who has experienced enemy encroachment on their land:

> *May you rise and secure your boundaries as the Father empowers you through the Son and by the Spirit. As you stop and allow Holy Spirit to breathe upon you, I pray the wind of Holy Spirit will refresh and empower you. May you experience His glory! If you feel as though you have lost your access to heaven and the enemy is pursuing you further outside the boundaries God intended for you, I decree that you will plant your feet! In Jesus' name, stop, face the enemy, and tell him that he must go—now! I loose an anointing for you to wear the victor's crown and be empowered in a new way! Amen.*

May you desire the revelation of God, and may its power remind you of who God is and who you are! May you and I always have access to God's heart so that we may gain strategies to prosper in all the fullness that God intended.

CHAPTER 5

EXPECT GOD!

Y OU HAVE A future! Jeremiah 29:11 (KJV) describes the *future* as "an expected end." The enemy hates your access to revelation about your future and resents your ability to see the world from God's perspective. God is magnificent, and the earth He created is filled with magnificence. However, without His Word and revelation, there would be no world and nothing glorious for us to experience. That is why revelation is so important.

Your expectations are part of your emotions. Expectations equate to hope, and hope leads to faith. If the enemy can bruise, wound, or destroy your expectations, you will lose hope and eventually your faith too. This will also cause you to lose vision—not physically but spiritually. This is a serious matter! Proverbs 29:18 (AMP) says, "Where there is no vision [no revelation of God and His word], the people are unrestrained; but happy and blessed is he who keeps the law [of God]."

IF THE ENEMY CAN BRUISE, WOUND, OR DESTROY YOUR EXPECTATIONS, YOU WILL LOSE HOPE AND EVENTUALLY YOUR FAITH TOO.

God's Word originates from within His being, unfolding all the elements and forces contained in our world. Psalm 33:6, 9 (AMP) says, "By the word of the LORD were the heavens made, and all their host by the breath of His mouth.... For He spoke, and it was done; He commanded, and it stood fast."

God sends His voice throughout the earth. Psalm 19:1–2 (AMP) says, "The heavens are telling of the glory of God; and the expanse [of heaven] is declaring the work of His hands. Day after day pours forth speech, and night after night reveals knowledge." When you are at the right place at the right time, you can hear what God has for you and know it is best. That is why the prophet Jeremiah said, "'For I know the plans and thoughts that I have for you,' says the LORD, 'plans for peace and well-being and not for disaster, to give you a future and a hope'" (Jer. 29:11, AMP).

Remember, Jeremiah prophesied this when God sent the people into Babylonian captivity. Being in captivity did not mean they could not hear from Him. Yes, God's people had to endure seventy years in Babylon, but they could still communicate with God. That fact should encourage us. We also live in a Babylonian society; however, that does not stop God from communicating with us about how to maneuver in the current age. The quality of His Word is extraordinary: It is like fire, a hammer, and life, enabling us to break through whatever the enemy or the world throws in our path. (See Jeremiah 23:29.)

EXPECTATIONS AND DESIRES

Your expectations can lead you into reality or into delusion. When you focus on a picture-perfect example of success, joy, and harmony, you want your life to naturally reflect the same. However, not everyone can experience an exemplary existence. Most of us have weathered misfortunes that we would love to see corrected. Many of us have inherited problems and habits that have been in our bloodlines before we were born. If we could only go back in time, rectify those issues, and enter the future with a clean slate!

YOUR EXPECTATIONS CAN LEAD YOU INTO REALITY OR INTO DELUSION.

I find that most people forget about the enemy of their souls and his efforts against them; Paul often addressed the opposition we face. In 1 Thessalonians 2:18 he shared what the enemy had been doing to oppose him and his ministry companions. In essence, the apostle asked the Thessalonian believers, "Have you forgotten who opposes you?"

Remember, we are in a war with this world, largely over all that is central to God's Word. The Word is equated with bread, and wars are usually waged for economic reasons or to satisfy human lust. James explained the dynamics of conflict in broad terms:

> What leads to [the unending] quarrels and conflicts among you? Do they not come from your [hedonistic] desires that wage war in your [bodily] members [fighting for control over you]? You are jealous and covet [what others have] and your lust goes unfulfilled; so you murder. You are envious and cannot obtain [the object of your envy]; so you fight and battle. You do not have because you do not ask [it of God]. You ask [God for something] and do not receive it, because you ask with wrong motives [out of selfishness or with an unrighteous agenda], so that [when you get what you want] you may spend it on your [hedonistic] desires.
>
> —JAMES 4:1–3, AMP

When expectations for our provision go unmet, we experience internal conflict. When we realize that someone or something in our environment is stopping up our supply, we experience external conflict. Often, we lose sight of who God is and what He can do in our lives. We forget that "the LORD is [our] Shepherd; [and we] shall not want" (Ps. 23:1).

Our unrestrained, unbridled, and lustful desires can cloud our vision of what God intended us to accomplish. Psalm 106:15 says, "He gave them their request, but sent leanness into their soul." Misguided desires can lead us to ask God for something other than His best, which can form the root of later conflicts—internally and externally. Misguided desires can also create disease and infirmity in our bodies.

Become aware of any desires that lead you astray and ask the Lord to align them with His. As Psalm 37:4 says, "Delight yourself also in the LORD, and He shall give you the desires of your heart"—just make sure your desires are also His.

ALIGNING YOUR EXPECTATIONS

Expect. Look at that word for a moment and say it aloud. Feel the weight and power of the word as it leaves your tongue and passes into the atmosphere around you. What you expect from life is often a direct result of your desires, whether they are prompted by Holy Spirit or not. *Expectation* can be defined as "a strong belief that something will happen or be the case in the future."[1] Not so surprisingly, *desire* is defined in much the same way, as "a strong feeling of wanting to have something or wishing for something to happen."[2]

Once, when I was preparing to speak about expectations, I asked my daughter to help me communicate this concept to the people who would hear the message. Here is what she wrote:

> As human beings, we are at odds constantly with our fleshly desires, our godly desires, and our limited understanding of destiny and time. We live in a world that blares the message of *following whims, doing what you feel,* and *creating your destiny*—without ever mentioning the Father's plan. In our quest to get what we hope for, it is very easy to get out of God's timing and miss destiny moments along the way.
>
> When I was younger, I had pretty strong opinions about what I was supposed to have, be, and become. OK, I'm just going to say it: I was stubborn. I thought I knew myself so well that I didn't need anyone else's input. Little did I know that God knew my heart better than anyone did, including me.
>
> At the beginning of life, when things are just getting going, it is so easy to get caught up in our own expectations, never looking to our Father to see whether they are part of His amazing plan. This happened in many ways as I walked through childhood and adolescence. But when I look back, one particular story comes to mind.
>
> One Christmas, like most kids, I had a very specific list of wishes. I spouted it off to anyone who dared ask me what

WHAT YOU EXPECT FROM LIFE IS OFTEN A DIRECT RESULT OF YOUR DESIRES, WHETHER THEY ARE PROMPTED BY HOLY SPIRIT OR NOT.

I wanted for Christmas, and I was very clear that these were the things I should be given. I wanted a doll, an Easy Bake Oven, and more clothes for my doll, Green Baby. Now, there was nothing wrong with my wants. They were normal expectations for a little girl. My brother, Daniel, who is three years older, also had a list of things he'd had his eye on. He wanted a Nintendo, a small TV to play it on, and an iguana. Looking at our two lists, his choices were more extravagant and odder than mine (I mean, really—an *iguana*).

So Christmas arrived, and I was filled with high expectations that my desires would be fulfilled. In my family, we open gifts on Christmas Eve, in a whole frenzy of laughter and eggnog. When the day came, and our gifts were handed out, I was given a set of diamond studs, a coat and watch, and a beautiful jewelry box. Meanwhile, Daniel received a TV, a Nintendo, and an iguana. He got an *iguana*!

You can probably picture my response. I threw down my watch and shoved aside the ornate jewelry box that would someday hold many prized possessions and trinkets of sentimental value, and stormed through the house. I was blazing mad, not to mention, completely determined to spoil Christmas for everyone.

For months, when I looked at Daniel's iguana or played on his Nintendo, I would get mad all over again. And why not? I had been so clear. There was no reason I shouldn't have gotten what I wanted; my list was so reasonable, useful, and normal. My parents tried to explain the gifts. Dad even went so far as to get me more jewelry to store in my jewelry box, but his act of love wasn't enough.

"But honey," he said, "these are things you can cherish."

"I don't want to cherish them," I pouted.

I couldn't see the outcome of those gifts or comprehend the reason I had gotten them. I had no foresight and concept of the future. All I could see was a dashed expectation and a hope deferred.

Oftentimes, when our expectation is not met, we are too stubborn and blind to see the gift God has presented us instead. Years later, while getting ready to leave my home in Texas for a strange new one in Colorado, I remember packing up that very well-used jewelry box, hardly remembering the time as a child when I didn't appreciate it. Fortunately for us, God has His expectations in line when it comes to His children.

One of my favorite movies as a kid was Disney's *The Little Mermaid*. In the story Ariel is the beloved daughter of King Triton. She is headstrong and gifted, but she has a very peculiar desire for a mermaid: She wants to be human. The song titled "Part of Your World" expresses this greatest desire of Ariel's. She knows it is not something her father agrees with; therefore, Ariel thinks he would not understand, let alone care about the desire of her heart.

Through a series of events, Ariel falls in love with a human prince. Meanwhile, a sorceress named Ursula wants to destroy King Triton at any cost. It seems she had once been a member of his court but had been banished many years before. (Sound like a familiar villain?) She turns Ariel into a human at the cost of Ariel's voice and the promise that Ursula will own her if Ariel is unable to live up to her side of the bargain. However, Ursula never intended for Ariel to live up to her side of the deal.

In the end Ursula is destroyed, but Ariel remains a mermaid. Her father, who loves her and knows that she is not meant to stay where she is, transforms her easily. Ariel discovers that her father was always able and willing to give her the desires of her heart, if she would have just waited.

We can be like unstable teenage mermaids sometimes. Often, we try to circumvent the Lord in the quest toward our destiny. We want to make it happen and, sometimes, we want to make it happen at any cost. Thankfully, God is ever faithful to teach His children good—though at times difficult—lessons.

In the business of our desires, the perilous areas for us humans are timing and choices. We think we know what we want, and we *expect* a clear path to obtaining it. Often, we don't see these choices and how they will affect our path. And we rarely see God's heart for us. All we know is something in us *wants*, and we have to go for it. We have hungry eyes that lock onto our goals like a homing beacon.

This kind of single-mindedness is great when applied to the things of the Spirit or the plans of the Father but not so good when applied to what the ego wants.[3]

I believe my daughter's words speak for themselves!

OUR DESIRE SHOULD BE TO EXPECT BLESSINGS

As previously mentioned, expectation is linked with desire, our human nature, and how we are made in God's image—spirit, soul, and body. Desire is a function of the soul that affects the human spirit.

When Eve ate the forbidden fruit, desire was the component of her soul most affected. God explained the consequences to her, saying, "I will greatly multiply your sorrow and your conception; in pain you shall bring forth children; *your desire* shall be for your husband, and he shall rule over you" (Gen. 3:16, emphasis added).

The soul of women shifted at that moment. In Hebrew the word *desire* suggests a stretching out after something that you wish for,[4] a deep longing for something that is driving your emotions. Although the ability to dethrone the serpent and take dominion over his voice was contained within the seed of the woman, she would have to learn to submit her soul's desire to God.

Jesus dealt with this issue when He taught His followers. Mark 9:35 says, "He sat down, called the twelve, and said to them, 'If anyone desires to be first, he shall be last of all and servant of all.'" He shared that each person would have to determine where their impulses were. They would have to learn to prefer others above themselves, and their intentions would have to realign with His purposes.

Desire is much more than a longing or demand. Our prayer life is developed through desire and the expectation of God's blessings. Yet our whole personality is wrapped up and dependent upon our desires being in submission. Misplaced desires can easily become covetous, leading to envy and jealousy. So when the soul submits to a sinful desire, our lives shift, we miss the mark of God's targeted plan for our life, and the soul falls to lust. (See Numbers 11:4–6.)

This lust creates an iniquitous pattern that affects all of society. We see all around us how a craving can be stimulated by the "desire to be rich" (1 Tim. 6:9). As Paul wrote, "The love of money is a root of all kinds of evil" (v. 10). Misplaced desire can also manifest in the imagining of illicit sexual acts, as Matthew 5:28 explains (regarding the committing of adultery in one's heart).

The desires of the flesh and our thoughts can lead us to destruction. When we gratify our flesh and satisfy our illegal desires, we open ourselves to many evils. Galatians 5:19–21 admonishes us with specifics:

> The works of the flesh are manifest, which are these; \ adultery, fornication, uncleanness, lasciviousness, idolatry, witchcraft, hatred, variance, emulations, wrath, strife, seditions, heresies, envyings, murders, drunkenness, revellings, and such like: of the which I tell you before, as I have also told you in time past, that they which do such things shall not inherit the kingdom of God.
>
> —GALATIANS 5:19–21, KJV

Peter shared a similar message:

> Therefore, since Christ suffered for us in the flesh, arm yourselves also with the same mind, for he who has suffered in the flesh has ceased from sin, that he no longer should live the rest of his time in the flesh for the lusts of men, but for the will of God. For we have spent enough of our past lifetime in doing the will of the Gentiles—when we walked in lewdness, lusts, drunkenness, revelries, drinking parties, and abominable idolatries. In regard to these, they think it strange that you do not run with them in the same flood of dissipation, speaking evil of you. They will give an account to Him who is ready to judge the living and the dead.
>
> —1 PETER 4:1–5

In the following passages, Peter continued in this vein:

> The Lord knoweth how to deliver the godly out of temptations, and to reserve the unjust unto the day of judgment to be punished: but chiefly them that walk after the flesh in the lust of uncleanness, and despise government. Presumptuous are they, selfwilled, they are not afraid to speak evil of dignities.
>
> —2 Peter 2:9–10, kjv

> Having eyes full of adultery, and that cannot cease from sin; beguiling unstable souls: an heart they have exercised with covetous practices; cursed children: which have forsaken the right way, and are gone astray, following the way of Balaam the son of Bosor, who loved the wages of unrighteousness; but was rebuked for his iniquity: the dumb ass speaking with man's voice forbad the madness of the prophet. These are wells without water, clouds that are carried with a tempest; to whom the mist of darkness is reserved for ever. For when they speak great swelling words of vanity, they allure through the lusts of the flesh, through much wantonness, those that were clean escaped from them who live in error. While they promise them liberty, they themselves are the servants of corruption: for of whom a man is overcome, of the same is he brought in bondage. For if after they have escaped the pollutions of the world through the knowledge of the Lord and Saviour Jesus Christ, they are again entangled therein, and overcome, the latter end is worse with them than the beginning. For it had been better for them not to have known the way of righteousness, than, after they have known it, to turn from the holy commandment delivered unto them.
>
> —2 Peter 2:14–21, kjv

If our desires are not submitted to the power of God's Spirit, we go haywire (as they used to say in East Texas when I was growing up). Hay wire kept entire bales of grass together after haying. But when the wire came loose, the whole bundle went every which way—it went *haywire*.

Desire is a function of emotion that causes us to look forward. Desire is also linked with the deep longing that can cause us to expect God to move on our behalf. Unless our desires are in check and submitted to God, our whole destiny can go haywire—splitting in many directions without being fully manifested in our lifetime, so let's focus our desires on the blessings of God.

EXPECTATION STRETCHES FORWARD

We know that desire and expectation are closely related, and both are mentioned in various contexts throughout Scripture. Expectation can be understood in several related ways, including the following:

- that which is looked for to come at a future time (Prov. 10:28)

- anticipation of something happening: a confident belief or strong hope that a particular event will happen

- a notion of something: a mental image of something expected, often compared to its reality or expected standard

- a standard of conduct or performance expected by or of somebody[5]

Expectation is a form of believing that what is not yet here is on the way.

Of the three Greek words translated "expect" in the English New Testament, *prosdokao* means "to expect, to wait for, to look for."[6] When you know something will likely or definitely happen, you release your emotions as if you are already watching for its manifestation. The outcome might not be all good, however, so you look ahead in either hope or dread. When prophets foretell the future, they can forewarn people of what is coming. But whatever they prophesy, they should convey an element of faith for the yet to be seen.

Another Greek word is *ekdechomai*, which appears in Hebrews 10:13 to express Jesus' period of "waiting till His enemies are made His footstool." In James 5:7 ekdechomai describes how the farmer waits "patiently" for "the precious fruit of the earth," to receive "the early and latter rain." Ekdechomai is also used in speaking of Abraham, who "waited for the city which has foundations, whose builder and maker is God" (Heb. 11:10).

Finally, the Greek word *apokaradokia* is translated "earnest expectation" in Romans 8:19 and Philippians 1:20. This word describes the stretching forth of the head toward something that is anticipated.[7] It is a fitting word for the time in which we live. Let's stretch forward as far as we can and expect God to stretch forth His hand to meet us!

However, in your expecting, keep this important key in mind: *Don't limit you with you!* One of the first statements the Lord ever spoke to me was "Do not lean on your own understanding! Trust in Me and you will see!" A great awareness accompanied this statement: I realized that my mind and abilities could limit God's actions through me, and I gained a deeper understanding of the reality that He lives *in me*.

After many years of ministry, counseling others, and watching people strive, I have concluded that most believers in the body of Christ are not fully aware of God's presence within them. This oversight has produced a great lack of confidence as we serve as His ambassadors. Instead of drawing on His life within us, we tend to rely on our own finite thinking and abilities. This prevents Elohim, the Creator, from fully expressing Himself beyond us.

However, this condition does not need to be permanent. Through meditation on Scripture and acts of faith, we can see Him in ways we have never seen Him before. He can transform our thinking so the world's limitations no longer confine us. We absolutely must become aware that He is living *in us*.

Remember, we are a corporate body in the earth realm. In the latter days, the Lord will have a strong people who do exploits. (See Daniel 11:32.) This means we will be a resourceful people. We will turn our resources into additional resources, and we will triumph over our enemies. However, we must move in expectation. We must remain aware of His living presence within us. We must see ourselves as His triumphant people.

UNLIMITED ACCESS TO ADVANCE ON YOUR PATH

As I embarked on a recent trip to Costa Rica, a preboarding announcement in Dallas alerted us to the fact that immigration into Costa Rica had become much more difficult since the previous year. When our plane landed, we entered the customs area. It was a sea of people.

The timing of our flight put us at the end of the line. As I stood there, I thought about all the things I had planned and needed to do. I knew the expected three-and-a-half-hour wait would hinder my assignment, but there was absolutely nothing I could do about it. So my assistant Aaron Smith and I entered the queue and waited. I looked up to heaven and said, "Lord, I am willing to wait in this line. You brought me here, and my time is in Your hands." Then I asked Aaron to agree that our steps would be ordered.

Anyone who knows me understands that I am quite capable of pushing through, getting things done, and pressing into my assignment. But on that day, I felt no unction to do any of those. I told Aaron that we needed to be patient and agree with the Lord's plans. Suddenly, an immigration officer came to where I was standing, lifted the rope without saying a word, and motioned for me to come with him. When I stepped beyond the rope, he immediately put it back into place, leaving Aaron behind it. Aaron said, "I am with him, and I have both passports!"

The official turned around, lifted the rope, and allowed Aaron to come with me. Still without saying a word, he brought us to the front of the diplomat line. By the Spirit, and in a moment's time, we had transcended the hindrance and passed through customs. Not one other soul received that privilege. The immigration officer said nothing. Yet somehow, the Lord Himself had pointed me out and directed the man to clear our path forward.

When I walked through customs, our host, Juanita Cercone (who is over Enlace, a Latin American, Christian-based broadcast television network), was in shock over our three-minute pass through customs! Aaron was also stunned, and I was amazed. Instead of relying on myself, I left the situation completely in the Lord's hands and watched Him work. He revealed Himself in me—not only to me but to the immigration officer, who submitted himself to God's will.

I said aloud, "Lord, why do we limit You so much? Why don't we quit striving and rely upon You in us to accomplish every purpose of our lives?"

I am still pondering that miracle.

YOUR VOICE OF AGREEMENT CAN PRODUCE ACCESS

Let me share another testimony about the power of speaking—one that is quite the opposite of our miracle in Costa Rica. Throughout most of my life, my ministry schedule has been very demanding. I have been in ten cities in eleven days, which gives you an idea of how intense my schedule can be.

Scheduling and staying on time are crucial in my line of work, and unexpected delays can wreak havoc on an itinerary. Shortly after 9/11, I was in California and had to catch an early morning flight to Arizona. Brian Kooiman assisted me on that trip, and although we arrived at the airport well ahead of our flight time, lines of people were everywhere. It was like a wall of passengers, and we could barely move forward.

At the rate we were moving, we would never make our flight. I looked at Brian and said, "Do something!"

Looking at the crowd surrounding us and seeing how far we had to go, he nervously asked, "What do you expect me to do?"

I looked at him and said, "If you don't do something now, we will miss our flight. *Do something!*"

For a second, I thought he would just stare helplessly back at me. But then something rose within him. He turned and shouted, "Famous person! Famous person! *Make way!*"

Evidently, it was exactly the right thing to say in Los Angeles. Everyone turned to look, and the crowd parted like the Red Sea. We immediately pushed toward our gate but then became stuck again.

I told Brian, "Say it again!"

He hesitated but looked toward our gate and shouted, "Famous person! Make way!"

Once again, the crowd parted and allowed us to move even closer to our gate. We repeated this several more times, until we reached the end of the terminal and caught our flight.

When Brian yelled into the atmosphere of that cultural setting, the culture submitted to the voice of God in him. In the airport chaos, I probably looked enough like Kenny Rogers to be taken for a "famous person," regardless of my true identity.

WHAT WE EXPECT FROM OTHERS

I am the parent of six children and have always worked with people, whether in human resources or ministry. I understand that how we expect others to perform can be either a blessing or a snare. Many times, we expect others to do what we do. This falls into the category of *an eye for an eye.* Unless we carefully manage, and even master, our expectations, we may become disappointed, judgmental, or critical. We must learn to assess someone's potential and encourage them to succeed in whatever God deems best for them.

Finding this balance is critical. Many children have been ruined by the unreachable expectations of their parents. Yet there is a fine line in this area—we must motivate our children to reach for the best, without demanding perfection of them or becoming overly disappointed when they regress or shrink back from success.

Our expectations in the workplace need to be balanced, as they play a role in shaping our coworkers' achievements. If someone wants to succeed, life is easier; the goal of a shared project is easier to accomplish and far more enjoyable. Conversely, if a coworker lacks self-motivated expectation, the group is still affected but in a less positive manner.

Personal motivation and the expectations of others powerfully impact groups. Four researchers conducted a study about *social loafing*—the tendency for people "to exert less effort on a task if they are in a group versus when they work alone."[8] As a general rule, people want to achieve. If they know someone is watching, they tend to work harder. The study showed that people with high achievement motivation (the tendency of an individual to work toward the achievement of personal goals or standards) tended to work hard regardless of how those around them performed. However, people with low motivation tended to pick up the slack and work harder when their peers did not work hard enough.[9]

MANY CHILDREN HAVE BEEN RUINED BY THE UNREACHABLE EXPECTATIONS OF THEIR PARENTS.

The study involved college students from the top or bottom 25 percent of their classes in achievement motivation. The students were paired off, not permitted to talk, prevented from monitoring each other's work rate, and told that the study was about "standardized communication" in the work environment.[10]

Students were then asked to come up with as many ideas as possible for the use of a common item. Unbeknown to them, the messages they supposedly exchanged with their partners were fake—some students were led to believe that their partners would try hard on the study, while others were told the opposite. Although the researchers could count how many ideas each person submitted, some students believed that only the total number of ideas produced per pair could be counted.[11] Thus, anyone prone to social loafing thought they could avoid detection.

From all possible combinations of factors, the study identified only one consistent loafer: students with low personal motivation who believed that their partners would work hard and that their own output could not be measured.[12] Because the subjects were college students, the study has implications for the emerging generation. But the lesson applies broadly: What we expect from others not only impacts their behavior but can raise or lower our own expectations and outcomes in life.

DO TEACHERS' EXPECTATIONS AFFECT STUDENT PERFORMANCE?

Jesus was a teacher. He was known in Nazareth as a carpenter. When Jesus was thirty years old, His Father in heaven activated the next portion of His call to redeem all mankind. This happened when He went into the wilderness and was baptized into the move of God that John the Baptist had been leading. (See Matthew 3:13–17.)

Upon Jesus' baptism, the heavens opened. Holy Spirit came down and led Jesus into the next dimension of revealing His identity: This was the temptation in the wilderness, where He resisted the tempter of all humankind. I believe that Jesus' resistance qualified Him for the next three years of ministry. After that, His first goal was to find those who would follow Him so He could teach them and impart His thought processes to the next generation and every generation to come. This three-year process was difficult, and Jesus sometimes questioned whether His students really understand His purpose. (See Matthew 16:5–12; Mark 8:17–21; John 14:9.)

When thinking generationally, everything we do that has historical impact should be delivered to and embraced by a generation able to understand and oversee the key developments that will impact the generation following them. With that in mind, I have worked with many gifted individuals and have had many disciples whom I was responsible for mentoring. I had to learn quickly not to give them the answers but to develop within them the ability to solve problems, think critically, and produce creative solutions. Thankfully, most of the disciples I mentored have succeeded in life.

Teaching is a solemn calling, and educating others is deeply entwined with expectations. *Expectation theory* is a concept relevant to many disciplines, and it explains how future expectations shape current behaviors. In relation to an educational program "based on expectation theory,"[13] here are some observations from key educators concerning their students:

The expectations teachers have for their students and the assumptions they make about their potential have a tangible effect on student achievement. Research "clearly establishes that teacher expectations do play a significant role in determining how well and how much students learn."

Students tend to internalize the beliefs teachers have about their ability. Generally, they "rise or fall to the level of expectation of their teachers....When teachers believe in students, students believe in themselves. When those you respect think you can, you think you can."

Conversely, when students are viewed as lacking in ability or motivation and are not expected to make significant progress, they tend to adopt this perception of themselves. Regrettably, some students, particularly those from certain social, economic, or ethnic groups, discover that their teachers consider them "incapable of handling demanding work."[14]

"Teachers' expectations for students—whether high or low—can become a self-fulfilling prophecy. That is, students tend to give to teachers as much or as little as teachers expect of them."[15] Most "highly effective teachers" adhere to uniformly high expectations. They "refuse to alter their attitudes or expectations for their students—regardless of the students' race or ethnicity, life experiences and interests, and family wealth or stability."[16]

In God's kingdom we must continue to expect the next generation to carry on His perfect will in the earth realm. When that expectation dissipates, I believe we will reach the end of an age. Holy Spirit is the third person of the Godhead, the leader of heaven's movement on the earth, and our Advocate, our Paraclete. A root word connected to the concept of the Paraclete is *praq*, part of the Aramaic word "*paraqleta*, which is taken from two root words: (1) *praq* 'to end, finish, or to save,' and (2) *lyta*, which means 'the curse.'" In other words, the Paraclete is the One who ends the curse that was begun in my house![17]

Holy Spirit will always expect a generation leading in God's kingdom plan to continue breaking the curses that would hinder

His house from being built. Holy Spirit also expects leaders in every generation to continue advancing and unleashing God's kingdom in the earth realm. Yeshua prophesied to Peter along these lines:

> I say to you that you are Peter, and on this rock I will build My church; and the gates of Hades (death) will not overpower it [by preventing the resurrection of the Christ]. I will give you the keys (authority) of the kingdom of heaven; and whatever you bind [forbid, declare to be improper and unlawful] on earth will have [already] been bound in heaven, and whatever you loose [permit, declare lawful] on earth will have [already] been loosed in heaven.
>
> —MATTHEW 16:18–19, AMP

Leaders are teachers because those they lead both follow their example and learn from their guidance. A valid expectation of every generation of leaders in God's kingdom is to see another generation—a next generation—pick up the baton and fulfill Holy Spirit's expectations. Specifically, Holy Spirit seeks those who will build, unlock, and advance God's kingdom and serve the plan of heaven in the earth realm.

As we expect from God, this is what He expects from us.

CHAPTER 6

LOOK AGAIN! THERE ARE SIGNS FOR YOUR FUTURE!

How do we look and see God on our path? Remember, the Jews waited for more than four hundred years for the Messiah to come. Yet, when He came, they had difficulty recognizing Him. We have a similar issue: Perhaps our greatest challenge is to recognize and see God's intervention as He accomplishes the ultimate purpose of our existence.

How I wish it were possible to awaken every human being's power to see God! Much of the issue, I think, involves knowing when we have encountered Him. How do we learn to see His signs on our path? How can the Scriptures prepare us to see Him and recognize Him for who He is?

Psalm 23 is a favorite passage among children who are being introduced to the Bible. Let me paraphrase the passage: "The Lord is the One on my path who leads me. He causes me to see what I need so I will not lack. If I follow Him and celebrate Him, I will see Him lead me through trials, wars, and even **THERE IS NO SUBSTITUTE FOR FAITH.** destruction. He will even prepare a table on which my enemies feed me. If I stay in His timing, He will go before me and follow me with His goodness and mercy. He will cause me to dwell with Him."

Many signs appear along our respective paths. However, seeing these signs and His presence requires faith. There is no substitute for faith: We prophesy according to our faith, and faith enables us to love. Yet faith works because we understand love. Scripture reveals that if we love God, we will see Him. (See Matthew 5:8; John 14:21.)

If we desire insight into our surroundings, we must grasp and live in a sense of awe about God. By knowing that He is, that He loves us, and that He has a will for our lives, we can let His will prevail, step by step. When we see Him, we will know when He calls us to turn this way or that. We are searching not for information or knowledge but for Him and for relationship. Our relationship with Him assuages the uncertainty that makes us unsure of the path, and it empowers us to follow Him as He reveals Himself to us. It is a matter of having eyes to see and ears to hear so that we acknowledge and cherish His presence and intervention in everything we attempt, occupy, and accomplish in life.

Clearly, the body of Christ must once again understand *signs*—those markers that identify and reveal the godly, redemptive plan of God in the world. We must not miss our signs or fear the supernatural. Instead, we need to enter the spiritual dimension that will lead us to our new "there." This process begins within each of us and ultimately becomes a collective demonstration, with signs serving as road markers along the way.

Signs are essential; they point us toward what God is accomplishing and become evident through objects and daily activities. These visible indicators bring us into agreement with God's path and purpose for the future. Wonders cause us to marvel by displaying God's supernatural activity, which may signify future events. God is purposeful about His signs and wonders, and He invites His people to ask for them. When He manifests through them, awe is the result!

A NEW PLACE

God performs new works in the heavenlies and brings what is new into our individual lives. Whether big or small, these developments—attitude tweaks, directions to new pathways, or clarified insights—forever change the course of our lives.

My entire life revolves around the concept of following God. Ever since I was introduced to Holy Spirit in 1972, I have been acutely aware of the Lord's presence on my path. I can honestly say that I have disciplined myself to seek Him in His Word daily. This fifty-year process has helped me perceive Him more readily than when I first began. Yet I know that there is more to perceive, and there are times still ahead when He will intervene in my life—times when I will see not only *Him* but the future He wants to reveal.

My first revelation after I was filled with Holy Spirit came in college, when the Lord spoke to me at a major young adult conference. In my spirit I perceived His voice and the words "I have called you for the healing of the nations." That divinely expressed purpose then became a reality for me. I cannot say I submitted fully or understood what He meant, but it was clear enough for me to trust that God's voice would direct me to accomplish it.

My path took several turns along the way. I served in corporate America, where I succeeded and greatly enjoyed my work. However, when God changed my course, I recognized it. I oversaw a large building project for a prominent church in the Houston area. Then the Lord led me to oversee the second-largest children's home in Texas. The path seemed unsettled at times, but I can honestly say that God led me.

Over the past fifty years, I have learned to recognize when a major encounter with God is imminent or necessary. One major shift came at the end of 1983—a year in which the Lord gave me a clearer direction toward missions. China had become a focus in my heart and spirit, and I served as the president of a mission group working in Beijing.

The Lord placed something additional in my heart: I had been praying intensely for the church in the Soviet Bloc, particularly in the Soviet Union. As I prayed, I saw the USSR church oppressed by seven straps that hindered the influence the Lord intended that church to have. Then the Spirit of God spoke to me and said, "I want the straps cut."

I entered an incredible time of prayer that night and went to bed ready to start a new year. Sometime after midnight, I awakened, and the Spirit of God visited and spoke to me. I wrote down everything He said over the next two hours, including a strategy for how He would free the church in the Soviet Union. He simply said, "Change of leadership," and He showed me that the third leadership change would happen as the church experienced an open window for advancement.

At breakfast the next morning, I told Pam the details of my visitation. Then I announced, "I must be called to the Soviet Union."

At the time Pam and I were administrators at the children's home I mentioned. I will never forget her response to my new calling: "You might be called to the Soviet Union," she said, "but I'm not. As a matter of fact, I was walking across the campus, and the Spirit of God told me that He is going to heal my body, and I am going to get pregnant."

Then she simply said, "This is going to be an interesting walk."

WHAT IT MEANS TO FOLLOW

With two clear but contrasting words from God, Pam and I knew that we had to seek the Lord's direction. In my quiet time that night, the Spirit of God quickened two words to me: "Follow Me."

We agreed to study what the Word says about following God, beginning in the Old Testament and the life of Abraham. God called him out from the worship of Molech (which is part of the Queen of Heaven system) and into worshipping the one true God. This brought Abraham into a blessing-filled covenant agreement with God.

After reading Genesis 12 and 15, Pam and I saw that we could enjoy the same blessings Abraham did, because as believers we are grafted into the same covenant. We realized that if we were to see these blessings manifested, we would have to follow God and worship Him in a new way. Just as Abraham left the familiarity and comfort of Ur, we would have to be willing to give up our traditions.

We also noticed a pattern that Jesus set when He called His disciples: They were to leave their homes, careers, families, friends, and old forms of religious practice, and they were to follow Him.

Some of the disciples had attended temple often, but others knew very little about worship. Jesus modeled a new way to worship: He went directly to the Father on their behalf and told them that they had access to the Father's will for their lives. I believe this established the biblical relationship between *going* and *worship*, which unlocks a person's destiny.

As Pam and I studied Jesus' model, the Lord quickened these words to me, "If you will learn to follow Me, you will see revival." Revival is a restoration of life that has been diverted into a process of death. I thought of Pam's womb and the church in the Soviet Union, and I believed that both would be revived!

SIGNS ALONG THE WAY

Pam and I knew we were hearing from God, but we did not know all the details. One night on our way to a prayer meeting at a Baptist church, we stopped for gas. As we drove away from the service station, we saw a large truck with two words on its rear: *Follow me.*

I saw this as a sign from the Lord and decided to follow the truck. When I drove closer, I could read the smaller lettering: Harpool Incorporated, Denton, Texas. Pam gave me the strangest look and explained, "I am reading a book called *Peace, Prosperity and the Coming Holocaust* by Dave Hunt.[1] The book isn't specifically about the Soviet Union, but it's dedicated to a missions group located in Denton, Texas, that works in the Soviet Union."

> **REVIVAL IS A RESTORATION OF LIFE THAT HAS BEEN DIVERTED INTO A PROCESS OF DEATH.**

That missions group was Mission Possible Foundation, Inc. I quickly decided to visit the organization's leaders and share with them the insights about the Soviet Union that I was receiving from Holy Spirit.

WORSHIP IN SPIRIT AND IN TRUTH

Mission Possible's leaders readily received me and listened to my concerns. That night Pam and I went to a conference hosted by

James Robison. God used the worship time to build this new work He was bringing about in our lives.

As we worshipped God, Pam and I expressed ourselves in different ways. I was exuberant, filled with overflowing joy, waving my hands because of the liberation God had brought into my life. Pam clearly understood the biblical principles of worship but was more reserved in expressing herself to the Lord. She seemed to worship in word, while I worshipped in spirit. That night I realized our marriage was marked by our unity in worship—"in spirit and truth" (John 4:24). Whenever we worship in unity of spirit and purpose, we enter the reality of God's purposes.

Pam saw it differently and made a curious observation, saying, "I only see two places in the New Testament where it talks about raising hands. You are so expressive in your worship that it has created problems for us."

I quickly replied, "I don't really care if the principle of raising hands is only in the concordance of the Bible. I only know that God has set me free, and I cannot keep myself from responding to that freedom."

Increasing the tension between the two of us, I then added, "If you ever become as desperate as I once was to allow God to accomplish what needs to be done, you'll probably express yourself in worship differently."

HEALING IN WORSHIP

When we returned to the conference the next day, I felt the presence of God surrounding us. I looked over at Pam, who had both hands in the air, waving them in worship. I gently asked, "What is happening with you?"

Amid the tears streaming down her face, she said, "The Lord is healing me!"

God's presence began to flow down through Pam's body. She said it felt like hot oil running through her veins. God's power expelled the clots from her uterus that endometriosis had caused! Two weeks later, Pam became pregnant—with twins! As she worshipped God, His power was released in her body in a whole new way. I eventually became executive director of the missions agency that was working in the Soviet Union. I remained a part of that organization until those seven straps were removed from the church in the Soviet Union and there was a window for evangelism to advance.

Pam and I followed God, learned to worship in a new way, and came into a new level of unity in our marriage. Worship broke the power of barrenness in our lives. God's anointing had broken the yoke! I truly believe that if we had kept doing things the same way, we would never have seen breakthrough into the new works God wanted for us. By following Him and seeing signs along the path, I ended up being initiated by the Lord into my call to the nations, and Pam ended up being healed, getting pregnant, and continuing to get pregnant over the next ten years. Miracles began to happen, and both our physical and spiritual inheritances were unlocked—because we saw a sign on the back of a truck that said *follow me*.

By 1990 I was in relationship with Mike and Cindy Jacobs of Generals International. Cindy then introduced me to Peter and Doris Wagner, whom God assigned to penetrate the world's most unreached people groups (the 10/40 Window). The Lord had initiated me into His original call on my life—the healing of the nations—and miracles happened as we journeyed throughout the world.

To this day Pam and I continually watch the Lord on our path. He instructs and reveals Himself because we remain in awe of who He is. We have seen Him do miracles in the process of raising our children, and I have watched Him do miracles throughout the world.

LEAVE FAMILY AND FOLLOW ME

All relationships are tested when covenant is involved. Abraham had to leave Ur of the Chaldees and then depart from Haran after his father, Terah, died. Jesus said several statements that seemed to challenge the family unit. For example, in Luke 14:26, He said, "If anyone comes to Me and does not hate his father and mother, wife and children, brothers and sisters, yes, and his own life also, he cannot be My disciple." (See also Matthew 19:29.) The family unit was so important to Jesus that He knew it would be a powerful consideration in discipleship. It was the strongest of all units on earth.

In Matthew's Gospel we find the most famous scriptures linked with war:

> Do not suppose that I have come to bring peace to the earth. I did not come to bring peace, but a sword. For I have come to turn "a man against his father, a daughter against her mother, a daughter-in-law against her mother-in-law—a man's enemies will be the members of his own household."
>
> —MATTHEW 10:34–36, NIV

Matthew 12 adds the following:

> While Jesus was still talking to the crowd, his mother and brothers stood outside, wanting to speak to him. Someone told him, "Your mother and brothers are standing outside, wanting to speak to you."
>
> He replied to him, "Who is my mother, and who are my brothers?" Pointing to his disciples, he said, "Here are my mother and my brothers. For whoever does the will of my Father in heaven is my brother and sister and mother."
>
> —MATTHEW 12:46–50, NIV

These statements seem hard, but the Lord is addressing the emotions of those who will follow Him and form family units that will endure persecution and future wars. Joseph H. Hellerman describes the believer's solidarity with the larger family—the church:

> Jesus of Nazareth publicly dissociates himself from his natural family, professes loyalty to a new surrogate family, and apparently expects his followers to do the same. It is this resocialization—at the kinship level—that marks early Christianity as distinct among the voluntary associations of Greco-Roman antiquity. The social solidarity characteristic of the family model, in turn, goes a long way to explain both the intimacy and sense of community so often cited as

unique to early Christianity, and the attractiveness of the early Christian movement to displaced and alienated urban-ites in the Greco-Roman world.[2]

If you are willing to leave your family unit to follow Christ, you will be known for your ultimate devotion. The church was to become a surrogate kinship group. Jesus never encouraged us to neglect family responsibility, as Luke 14:26 might seem to indicate. Let me paraphrase that verse and focus on the essence of what I believe He was saying: "If you have any emotional tie that you are exalting above Me, I cannot teach you what you need to know as you enter the season ahead of you!"

Family is a mighty war unit, and nothing is as strong as a whole family bloodline submitted to the Lord, exalting Him, and honoring His priorities.

HOW FAR WILL YOU FOLLOW?

Before we discuss Jesus and His supernatural demonstrations, let's look at Abraham, the father of faith into whom we have been grafted. God is the God of Abraham, Isaac, and Jacob. He is the God of Israel. In response to his God and to strengthen his faith, Abraham submitted to a lengthy process of learning to know God and being tested.

At one point God cut covenant—an agreement—with Abraham. It was a true covenant, in which God essentially said, "Abraham, your battles are My battles."

> **IF YOU ARE WILLING TO LEAVE YOUR FAMILY UNIT TO FOLLOW CHRIST, YOU WILL BE KNOWN FOR YOUR ULTIMATE DEVOTION.**

That is the nature of being in covenant with the Lord. We can experience peace because we are confident of His backing. When He calls us to obey, we can trust Him without reservation. We have already discussed Abraham's final and most drastic test—when Elohim commanded him to sacrifice Isaac. Abraham's choice to bind Isaac on the altar represented the total submission of two generations to the will of God. Abraham lifted his eyes, and vision for the future was opened to him. The prophetic word (to add to what God had spoken before) was released again.

When we are in covenant with the Lord, we can see our provision. We don't need to figure out how God will keep His promises. We don't even need to understand why He chooses to accomplish His will in unusual ways. We need to remain in covenant with Him, knowing that whatever He asks or does will only be for our best and His glory. When this is our perspective, we can stay focused on worship and on His goodness—and from that vantage point, we can see Him, recognize His signs, and be confident of our next step.

If we remain faithful and refuse to cower in fear or distrust, we can see miracles that demonstrate God's power in our lives. It is as simple as seeing clearly, by the power of His Spirit. Then, as we obey, He extends into the future the promise He has already made.

MIRACLES, THE SUPERNATURAL, AND PONDERING

Miracles are linked with God's power—His inherent ability to come from the supernatural realm into the natural one and rearrange events, time sequences, and established orders. Miracles are not contrary to nature; they simply bring nature into harmony with God's purpose. Human knowledge and ability offer only a limited perspective of God's workings. He performs miracles to help us comprehend higher laws that we have either missed or strayed from in the process of living. His miracles also attract the unsaved to our powerful God.

The word *miracle* is linked with the principle of wonder; therefore, it is necessary to have a sense of awe when it comes to God. Miracles are the wonderful events that only He can conceive in heaven, and He invites us to witness these supernatural manifestations in our world! As natural events become subservient to divine power, special revelations of God's presence and power are displayed. This release of power establishes and preserves His will and the life processes of human flesh while extending eternity into our world and walk.

Jesus didn't perform miracles merely to attract our attention; He wanted to demonstrate Father's heart at key times and places to change the thought processes of those who witnessed His works. Of course, the first and most incredible miracle was His incarnate birth, and I love the scriptural prophecies surrounding this event. After His birth and circumcision (a sign of covenant), Joseph and Mary presented Jesus at the temple, where Simeon, a devout and aged man who recognized the baby as the long-awaited Messiah, "took [Jesus] up in his arms...blessed God" and prophesied of things to come (Luke 2:8–32). Luke 2:33 says that Joseph and Mary "marveled at" Simeon's prophecy.

> **MIRACLES ARE NOT CONTRARY TO NATURE; THEY SIMPLY BRING NATURE INTO HARMONY WITH GOD'S PURPOSE.**

This was like Mary's reaction when the shepherds came to see the infant Jesus. Luke 2:19 says she "pondered...in her heart" the words she heard. The idea is that she reflected on and absorbed them, much as a cow digests its food. Cows have four stomach compartments, and every bite is digested progressively in each of these compartments until it is thoroughly broken down and absorbed into the bloodstream. This parallels Mary's processing of the prophetic words she heard. When she meditated on the words, they went deep down into her bone marrow and became part of her being. They clarified her vision, just as God clarifies our vision so we can see Him.

THE PROCESS OF SEEING CLEARLY

Just as Jesus moved through a process from His birth to the initiation of His earthly ministry, we undergo a process and witness the fullness of God's plan progressively, over a period. A process can be described as "the course or method of continuing development that involves change."[3] It is also the orderly movement that takes a person from one place to another. Anatomical processes are structural "projections or outgrowths" of bones that "serve as attachment sites for muscles, tendons, and ligaments."[4]

Processes can prepare something or someone for special treatment. Here is a portion of the process Jesus underwent following His birth:

1. Matthew 3:13–17: Jesus had to identify with John's message and be baptized into the existing wineskin— John's baptism of repentance. This opened the heavens and gave Him vision for Father's will for the future. (Eventually, Jesus' message would go beyond John's and require a new wineskin and baptism.)

2. Matthew 4:1–11: Jesus was initiated into the wilderness warfare that enabled Him to overcome every temptation of the enemy, both in that encounter and as a model for our lives.

3. John 1:35–46: Jesus found followers seeking true relationship who would carry on His message once He completed Father's will here on earth. Andrew, his brother Simon (Peter), and Philip became followers. Philip and Andrew had been following John the Baptist, but they transferred from his wineskin into Jesus' wineskin.

4. John 2:1–11: Jesus' mother Mary encouraged Him to perform His first miracle at a wedding in Cana. Such wedding celebrations often lasted for seven days. During the wedding, the wine ran out, so Mary asked Jesus to supply more wine. (According to John 5:19, Jesus only did what His Father was doing, so we can assume that this miracle aligned with the Father's will.)

   Jesus took six purification pots, had them filled with water, and then turned the water into wine. This miracle helped His disciples believe in a new way, and His glory began to be seen in the earth realm.

5. Matthew 5:3–12; 8:1–13: Jesus preached the Beatitudes. Afterward, He demonstrated His preaching by healing a leper. At the same time, a very significant healing occurred—the healing of the centurion's servant. The centurion recognized the power and authority of Yeshua's words. Therefore, the Lord said of him, "I have not found such great faith, not even in Israel!" (Matt. 8:10).

6. Matthew 8:23–27: Jesus continued to demonstrate His authority to His disciples by commanding nature to realign. He rebuked the winds and waves of the sea. This caused His frightened disciples to see His authority in a new way.

7. Matthew 8:28–32: Jesus arrived in the country of the Gadarenes, where a demon-possessed man had long blocked people from entering. Jesus cast the demons into a herd of pigs, demonstrating His power over demonic spirits.

8. Mark 1:21–28: Jesus demonstrated His power in a synagogue by casting out a demon from a man who was in attendance. This shocked the "religious church" of that day.

9. Matthew 9:1–8: Jesus healed a paralytic man by forgiving his sins, which jarred the religious community. They could receive the grace to heal, but they rejected the grace to extend forgiveness.

10. Matthew 13:3–9: Jesus prophesied and illuminated His teachings through parables. One of the greatest

parables involved seed, a sower, and the fruit that was produced. This parable helps hearers understand the power of the Word of God going deep within us.

11. John 8:1–11: Jesus broke religious custom by extending grace to a woman found in adultery. His actions confronted the hypocrisy of the temple's male leadership, and the woman became a remarkable example to the society around her.

12. Matthew 13:24–53: Jesus taught the kingdom of heaven through a series of parables, including the parables of the wheat and tares, the mustard seed, the leaven, the hidden treasure, the pearl of great price, the dragnet, and the householder. These teachings, along with His life, revealed the kingdom of heaven in the earth realm and helped people recognize its power within them to transform their surroundings.

13. Matthew 14:13–21: Jesus demonstrated the law of multiplication based on the law of use. He took what was available—a young boy's lunch—and used it to feed thousands, with much food left over.

14. Matthew 28:1–8: Jesus overcame death, hell, and the grave! Witnesses testified to the victorious power of His resurrection.

15. John 20:22: Jesus breathed on His disciples, releasing Holy Spirit and preparing them for their future roles as apostles.

16. Matthew 28:18–20: Jesus extended a future call to His disciples to go forth and spread His good news throughout the world.

17. Luke 24:50–53: Jesus ascended. This demonstrated the Father's power to seat believers for future ruling and reigning.

18. Acts 2:14–39: Jesus' disciples overcame fear and began to share and demonstrate His message in the world.

19. Acts 3:2–10: Peter and John healed a man at the Gate Beautiful. Those who witnessed this miracle became aware of an ecclesia that appeared to challenge the political authorities of that day.

20. Revelation 2 and 3: Nearly seventy years after Jesus' ascension, He visited the seven churches named in the Book of Revelation via a message that He revealed to the apostle John.

"Jesus Christ is the same yesterday, today, and forever" (Heb. 13:8). We are called not only to do what He did but to do "greater works" (John 14:12). In the current season, I believe that we are moving into a greater understanding of God's kingdom. To live according to the culture of God's kingdom in the days ahead, we will find new ways of communicating and demonstrating His power.

Dissatisfaction with traditionalism is widespread today, and people are seeking truth and power. Therefore, God will shift many people into new places to reveal His glory and kingdom more fully. We must recognize the signs on our path, and we must also understand the times and the age and follow the patterns that He showed to us.

Recognize provision—see Jehovah Jireh

When reflecting on Abraham's test—regarding Isaac's sacrifice—and the process that he entered, I am reminded of where we are today. Everyone is in a process of some sort, but if we keep faith as we go, we will develop clear vision for the future. Remember,

God revealed Himself to Abraham as Jehovah Jireh, the One who causes you to see your provision. So *Jireh* is a seeing word.

As we seek God in this season, *seeing* becomes one of the most important words to understand. Jehovah Jireh says, "I have provision for you to see." In Genesis 22:7, when Isaac was curious about where the lamb was, he eventually saw the sacrifice God had provided. Provision is linked with seeing. Yet I believe that we can see beforehand—or before the need arises—in which case, prevision and provision are essentially the same concept.

The Old Testament word *roeh* speaks of a prophet as a seer who can open provision. But location is also key. Mount Moriah was the place God ordained and chose. Therefore, that is where Abraham would find God's provision—a ram that was waiting to be seen and sacrificed. This unfolding of events became a prototype of God's provision of His only Son, who was sacrificed for us. (See John 1:29; 1 Peter 1:18–19; Revelation 5:11–13; Romans 8:32; John 3:16.)

Look again—your provision is there!

When our eyes are open, God can reveal His supernatural ability to provide for us. Let me share an amazing testimony of God's ability to keep what we have committed to Him. Janice Swinney, one of the pastors and administrators at Glory of Zion International, experienced an outright intervention by God that will encourage you to see what the Lord has for you.

> My father has been gone for eleven years, and I have had little contact with his wife since his death. On March 8 of this year, I received word of my stepmother's death. She and my father were married for twenty-four years and were both blessings to their children and grandchildren. In preparation of their passing, my father and stepmother established a living trust with my older brother as the grantor trustee. The estate was a combination of assets that my father (and mother) had accumulated throughout their lifetimes, as well as property that my stepmother had inherited from her parents. Over the last twenty years, there has been much prayer

going up regarding this particular inheritance, partially due to some unresolved issues in this blended family. Upon my stepmother's death, I called my spiritual authorities, Chuck and Keith Pierce, discussed the change that had occurred in my life, and asked for prayer. Both Chuck and Keith spoke into the situation. So many times when the Lord hears our prayers, He starts working, but we must *look* to see Him in our midst.

On March 10, while I was sitting at my desk at 2:50 p.m., the Lord spoke to me and said, "Go now and get some cash to pay Joshua Awbrey back for your lunch." Immediately, I left the office and drove to the RaceTrac Gas Station near the church. I used the ATM to get fifty dollars in cash (two twenties and one ten-dollar bill). I then went inside, purchased a Diet Coke, and handed the cashier the ten-dollar bill. He gave me change of nine dollars and some coins.

I returned to the office, and as I was counting out the eight dollars to pay Josh, I saw that one of the dollar bills had handwriting in ink on the front of it. I *looked again* and became completely speechless! My father's name—last and first—and the number 768 were written on one of the dollar bills. At first, I was overcome with amazement and awe. This was so supernatural. Only God could have orchestrated this moment!

I was so excited! I then reached for my phone to call Keith Pierce and give him the testimony of the sign. I was only giving the high points. Then I said, "Oh, Keith, there is also a number written here—it is 768. What does that mean?" He answered with, "I'll call you back."

In less than five minutes, he called back and told me the Lord had said to look at the seventh book (Judges) in the sixth chapter and the eighth verse. That verse (KJV) says, "That the LORD sent a prophet unto the children of Israel, which said unto them, Thus saith the LORD God of Israel, I brought you up from Egypt, and brought you forth out of the house of bondage—I continued into verse 9—and I delivered you out of the hand of the Egyptians, and out of the hand of all that oppressed you…and gave you their land."

As I was praising and thanking the Lord for this supernatural sign of the assurance of my inheritance, I heard the Lord laugh. He said, "It is My pleasure to give you the kingdom. Just believe. Do not allow a cap to come over your faith by trying to imagine how I will do a thing. *Just believe that I AM!*"

While pondering the path of this, I realized how incredible the timing of each step was. Being at the right place—in this case the exact cashier at the RaceTrac, at the right time—[and] moving with the voice of the Lord were as supernatural to seeing the sign as the sign itself. This situation gave me a great deal of respect for those Israelites at that first Passover who stayed under the blood covering until the sign of deliverance came.[5]

Look again—God is there! He will give you the signposts, pointing you in the right direction and changing your life in a moment. The Lord is guiding you into a new season, so this is a perfect time for you to war your way into the promised inheritance of your future.

Expect Him to perform His Word

The Lord is always looking for a generation of leaders. He is looking for individuals who will *expect* Him to perform His Word! When He finds such people and sees their faithfulness to lead, He reiterates His plan for them to prosper. When the time is right, God will manifest His blessings to them. Here is what God said to Joshua, the son of Nun, when His time to manifest the promise had come:

Moses My servant is dead; now therefore arise [to take his place], cross over this Jordan, you and all this people, into the land which I am giving to them, to the sons of Israel. I have given you every place on which the sole of your foot treads, just as I promised to Moses. From the wilderness [of Arabia in the south] and this Lebanon [in the north], even as far as the great river, the river Euphrates [in the east], all the land of the Hittites (Canaan), and as far as the Great

[Mediterranean] Sea toward the west shall be your territory. No man will [be able to] stand before you [to oppose you] as long as you live. Just as I was [present] with Moses, so will I be with you; I will not fail you or abandon you. Be strong and confident and courageous, for you will give this people as an inheritance the land which I swore to their fathers (ancestors) to give them. Only be strong and very courageous; be careful to do [everything] in accordance with the entire law which Moses My servant commanded you; do not turn from it to the right or to the left, so that you may prosper and be successful wherever you go. This Book of the Law shall not depart from your mouth, but you shall read [and meditate on] it day and night, so that you may be careful to do [everything] in accordance with all that is written in it; for then you will make your way prosperous, and then you will be successful. Have I not commanded you? Be strong and courageous! Do not be terrified or dismayed (intimidated), for the Lord your God is with you wherever you go.

—Joshua 1:2–9, amp

Let me prophesy to you from the previous passage:

The time has come to get up and move into what I have for you. The past leadership has passed; you sat under their training and gleaned from them. However, there were things I wanted to do on their behalf that they never allowed Me to accomplish. Now rise up! I will give you both the wilderness and the richness of the territory. I will give you every enemy within the territorial boundary that I have promised. I have been waiting for you to step into these blessings. The blessings are in your blood. Your bones cry out for what I have to give you. Your heart is filled with desire for what I have promised you. Be confident in what I have done within you! *Expect Me* to work on your behalf. Align your desires with My desires for you. My desires are best. I have already promised your father and mother what I would do, so you expect Me to do this now!

Do not violate My boundaries. Walk wisely and circumspectly before Me, and you will prosper. Meditate and chew on

My words to you, and you will succeed. You will see your way as a prosperous way—not one cursed and littered with death and destruction. You will have good success if you expect Me to move on your behalf. Let this word invigorate you. My vigor will dispel fear. Enter in now, and allow Me to guide you daily. No enemy on your path can stop you. You will know when to stop and when to go! Expect to hear Me daily and feel My presence directing you. *Expect Me!* Now is your time to think like Me and occupy your promise. As you occupy, you will see!

OCCUPY YOUR IDENTITY, LAND, AND ATMOSPHERE

Our atmosphere is impregnated with regional culture, unbelief, and doubt. Each of our voices impacts our atmosphere. To stay aligned with God's timing and gain access, we must hear what to say and when to say it. If we allow the enemy to rule our atmosphere, he will. When God promised Abraham the boundaries of His covenant in Genesis 15:18–21, He included all the enemies who not only occupied the land but held the atmosphere hostage. These resistant forces had to be driven out for the Promised Land to be everything God intended.

The same is true for God's promises to us. We must occupy whatever territory God gives us, and we must defend it against all hostile forces. Our mandate to occupy begins in our Father's throne room and extends not only to the earth on which we walk but all the way to hell. Consider the following: When you own a piece of property and have a deed of ownership, you own that property from heaven to earth. If you steward the property well, all the minerals, water, and everything in the land will produce fullness. You can sell your mineral rights. You can sell your water. But prospering the land requires unlocking all its blessing and establishing your rule of ownership in the atmosphere.

So here is a prayer principle we must grasp: *On earth as it is in heaven.* We are in a war not only over the land but over the atmosphere. When Jesus began demonstrating His Messiahship, He returned to Nazareth, the place of His upbringing. Mark 6:5–6 explains that He could do few miracles there because of the atmosphere. Think about it: Even God Himself could not break through the atmosphere, because people were so familiar with who they thought Jesus was that they could not receive the demonstration of His Messianic identity.

We need to occupy our identity, territory, and atmosphere. When we fully embrace our identity and authority in the Lord, we can exercise them and give the earth and all the territory's inhabitants an opportunity to align or realign with God and His kingdom.

KNOW THE GOLIATH THAT IS RULING YOUR ATMOSPHERE

I love the story of King David's throne—the legacy and heritage is so powerful. David, chosen from the tribe of Judah during a time of chaos and confusion, was promised by God that he would rule over Israel. Picture this scene: a young shepherd boy—the youngest of eight brothers—receiving a prophecy of such magnitude!

God saw David as king from the start, but David had to endure a lengthy process before occupying the throne. When God spoke to David through Samuel, David began to see himself as royalty as well. Because David believed God and embraced the identity God gave him, he was able to gain that perspective. To withstand the struggles and occupy the throne, David had to first see himself as God saw him—in the ultimate God-ordained plan for his life.

Let's talk about atmosphere a little more. David was watching the flocks while his brothers warred against the Philistines. Then his father essentially said, "You need to take provision to your brothers on the battlefield." (See 1 Samuel 17:17–18.) As assignments go, delivering provision doesn't seem very special. But even the most mundane assignments can open your future and your destiny.

When David arrived at the battlefield, he saw how fiercely Goliath controlled the atmosphere. For forty days the giant "impregnated" Israel's troops with fear by hurling at them words of unbelief and defeat. David was astounded to find Israel's troops agreeing with what Goliath prophesied. But that is how bullies rule: They invade the atmosphere and cause their victims to believe what they say and think what they think.

David looked at Goliath and listened to his words, knowing that the giant should have been taken out long ago, when the Promised Land was conquered. Yet now, Goliath not only intimidated God's people but also challenged God. So in 1 Samuel 17:26, David provoked Israel's soldiers and essentially asked, "Why are you listening to this?"

Israel's soldiers were clearly terrified of the giant and his decrees. But David saw the situation differently. He knew he belonged to God, and he recognized himself as God's ambassador. Therefore, he never came into agreement with Goliath's decrees. Nor did he feel threatened by Goliath's stature. Instead, he was confident of God's backing and saw an opportunity to bring the giant to account.

THAT IS HOW BULLIES RULE: THEY INVADE THE ATMOSPHERE AND CAUSE THEIR VICTIMS TO BELIEVE WHAT THEY SAY AND THINK WHAT THEY THINK.

First Samuel 16:14 reveals an important shift in Israel's situation: The Spirit of Adonai had "departed from Saul," who was in charge of the army and all of Israel. Meanwhile, David was being drawn to step up: The word Samuel had spoken when he anointed David as king seemed to become active, and the promise of canceled taxes and marriage to Saul's daughter further motivated David to silence the voice that threatened Israel.

So in 1 Samuel 17:32, David volunteered to fight Goliath. Saul accepted his offer, dressed him in the king's armor, and sent him up against this giant. (See 1 Samuel 17:38.) However, in verse 39, David refused to wear Saul's armor, preferring to occupy his own identity in the midst of the battle. So David dressed as himself and used his own weapon of choice—a slingshot. With one small stone, he silenced Goliath, entered a whole new dimension of his life, and opened a new future for Israel!

A SEASON OF DETHRONING OUR GOLIATHS

We are living in a new historical era. In our times, as in any other period, we must accept and own our responsibility to dethrone anything from the past that would hinder the advancement of God's kingdom. This is key, because advancing in the present season also secures our future season.

For our discussion let's see Goliath not only as a biblical and historical figure but as a ruling giant who exerts atmospheric control in our lives. That giant is working to saturate our atmosphere with fear and defeat, but we must remember that the Lord has planned for us to triumph. He has summoned us to dethrone our Goliaths!

Therefore, two key principles of atmospheric control are essential: First, discern the thought processes that have infiltrated any space entered. If they are contrary to heaven's will, take responsibility to change the atmosphere. Remind yourself of who you are in Christ and act accordingly. The enemy is always scheming, but remember, as God's ambassador, you are sent into every atmosphere you encounter. Second, remember your ultimate goal and reason for being in that place. Discern God's perspective on your mission, discover your role, and seek understanding of your calling to complete your assignment.

Be aware of another issue: familiarity. Does the atmosphere seem too familiar? Do the enemy's plots seem like repeat performances from past struggles? Is everything so familiar that you cannot recognize the new thing God is trying to do? Does the atmosphere seem like leftovers from the last season? Is it aligned with the world's mentality rather than with heaven's will?

Dethroning the giant requires spiritual awareness and the discipline to keep your expectations in line with Holy Spirit. Asking yourself the following questions will help you:

1. Do I have an expected end? (What is it?)

2. Can I see the next step in that direction?

3. Am I afraid of overreaching my goal?

4. Is stress keeping me from mounting up for the cause?

5. What is my confidence level, and is my confidence in myself or in God?

6. Have I developed a spirit that is different from that of the world? (Remember Joshua, Caleb, and Daniel: They did not operate in the spirit of the world or the religious structures that encompassed them.)

To respond to your Goliath effectively, keep looking, know that God is on the path with you, and be mindful of His signposts. Develop an understanding of what is happening within you, and do the following:

1. If you feel weak, stop and ask the Spirit of God to show you whose armor you are wearing. (Make sure it is yours!)

2. Ask the Lord to fortify your shield of faith.

3. Look again, and expect victory!

CHAPTER 7

A TIME TO WAR: VISITATION, DREAMS, AND THE POWER OF GOD'S REVELATION

A S I PONDER the times in which we live, I am struck by how the nations revolve around Israel. Yet the most influential powers—China, Russia, and America—dominate the world stage. The question remains: Which of these three will truly "win gold" by satisfying God's heart and honoring His covenant with Israel?

As I watched the 2024 Olympics, everything I had carried in my heart for the previous forty years came to mind. In 1984 I started working with an organization that helped sustain the church during religious oppression in the Soviet Bloc. I also worked with a group of professionals who helped develop systems that would open communications between China and America. This was not a covert operation but rather a moment that presented itself when President Reagan formed a new relationship with China.[1] Unfortunately, the window lasted only until the Tiananmen Square protests and massacre in 1989.

I carried all three nations in my heart, in part, because the Lord had assigned me to pray for the world's three major powers. This assignment was beyond anything I could have imagined being given. I would love to say I understood why God entrusted me with it, but I didn't. I only knew what He told me in 1972: "I have called you for the healing of the nations." In my finite mind, I assumed He would eventually assign me as a missionary to a particular nation. However, I had never submitted fully to the "nations" call.

During the 2024 Summer Olympics, I took the gold medal count as a sign. As the count shifted back and forth between America and China, the count ended up tied at forty—an apt picture of where we stand worldwide as America and China dominate and Russia strives to regain the strength and resources it lost during the 1980s and 1990s.

I believe Russia's diminished strength is exactly why Ukraine is a battlefield today. I visited Ukraine in 2008, and my prediction of this outcome is documented. Meanwhile, China continues to develop strength and control measures, while America fights to maintain the worldwide authority and influence it amassed in recent centuries.

FOCUS: THE PROPHETIC WORD DIRECTS OUR STEPS

This chapter is about how the prophetic word of the Lord leads God's people forward. Most importantly, my goal is to help you understand how you war with your prophetic word, which is essential for fulfilling your God-intended destiny. You can start by personalizing 1 Timothy 1:18–19 (NLT), as I did: It says, "[Chuck], here are my instructions for you, based on the **PROPHETIC** prophetic words spoken about you earlier. May **REVELATION** they help you fight well in the Lord's battles. **ALWAYS BEGINS** Cling to your faith in Christ and keep your conscience clear." **WITH YOU.**

In the remaining chapters, I want to show you how to watch and war with the prophetic words that will lead you beyond 2026 and into the future. Remember, you do not war against those prophetic words; you keep God's words within you as you wage war. Prophetic revelation always begins with you. You—and your destiny—play a major role in the church's corporate alignment with God. This alignment and the kingdom government (of which you are a part) affect the territory in which you live. This includes your land, city, state, and nation. The prophetic word with which you do battle is about you, how you received from the generation before you, and how you pass it to the two generations that follow. Isaiah reminds us of the following:

> "As for Me, this is My covenant with them," says the LORD: "My Spirit which is upon you [writing the law of God on the heart], and My words which I have put in your mouth shall not depart from your mouth, nor from the mouths of your [true, spiritual] children, nor from the mouth of your children's children," says the LORD, "from now and forever."
> —ISAIAH 59:21, AMP

When the four generations—ours, the one before us, and the two after us—are aligned and declaring the will of heaven over God's covenant plan, His glory comes. We must know the prophetic word the previous generation has been warring so we can learn to war with those promises and also teach them to the generations that follow us. Each generation must develop their testimony of God's faithfulness as they rehearse the Word of the Lord.

> Arise [from spiritual depression to a new life], shine [be radiant with the glory and brilliance of the LORD]; for your light has come, and the glory and brilliance of the LORD has risen upon you. For in fact, darkness will cover the earth and deep darkness will cover the peoples; but the LORD will rise upon you [Jerusalem] and His glory and brilliance will be seen on you.
> —ISAIAH 60:1–2

The contents of this book are meant to help you war well. My desire is for you to triumph—along with God's corporate kingdom, the place in which you dwell, your nation, and the generations that follow you.

WARRING WITH YOUR PROPHETIC WORDS FOR A MANIFESTATION

The Word of God endures forever. (See Isaiah 40:8; Psalm 119:89.) The world cannot overcome the power of God's life-giving Word when it is released through the spirit of man. The Spirit of God breathes on the Word and gives it life and power. His Word is not bound by time but transcends the generations. The deeds initiated by the Word, shared by one person, can affect the generations to come. The Word produces works, including divine revelation and outcomes that we believe will manifest. The Word is synonymous with *speech, command, promise,* and *prophecy.* Therefore, we must speak the Word or utter our belief. Prophetic utterance releases vision, and "where there is no vision [no redemptive revelation of God], the people perish" (Prov. 29:18, AMPC). The Word releases vision; vision produces faith and contains the allotment for our provision.

An example of warring for a manifestation is seen in what the Lord spoke to the prophet Ezekiel:

> Prophesy and say to the hills and mountains, dales and valleys of Israel: "This is what the Lord God says! I am full of fury because you suffered shame before the surrounding nations..... I will honor my great name, that you defiled, and the people of the world shall know I am the Lord. I will be honored before their eyes by delivering you from exile among them. For I will bring you back home again to the land of Israel.
>
> "Then it will be as though I had sprinkled clean water on you, for you will be clean—your filthiness will be washed away, your idol worship gone. And I will give you a new heart— I will give you new and right desires—and put a new spirit within you. I will take out your stony hearts of sin and give you new hearts of love. And I will put my Spirit within you so that you will obey my laws and do whatever I command.
>
> "And you shall live in Israel, the land which I gave your fathers long ago. And you shall be my people, and I will be your God. I will cleanse away your sins. I will abolish crop

failures and famine. I will give you huge harvests from your fruit trees and fields, and never again will the surrounding nations be able to scoff at your land for its famines."

—EZEKIEL 36:6, 23–30, TLB

I believe this passage describes *aliyah*—the return to Israel of Jews from the diaspora—which started at the end of World War II, escalated in the 1960s, and continues to this day. It has not been an easy process. Much war and struggle have been required for this prophecy to manifest. The war for this prophecy's fulfillment started immediately after God spoke to Ezekiel.

When God speaks a prophecy, its manifestation does not begin immediately. Realizing this is crucial as you war for your prophetic destiny, your effect on the world, and your participation in God's work. Ezekiel's prophetic journey is instructive in this regard, revealing a five-step process to secure the prophetic word from the heavenlies and decree it into the atmosphere of the world—including the current world. Warring with your prophetic word always precedes God's performance of that word.

WARRING WITH YOUR PROPHETIC WORD ALWAYS PRECEDES GOD'S PERFORMANCE OF THAT WORD.

Once God gave Ezekiel the vision of the valley of dry bones (see Ezekiel 37), the process of prophetic fulfillment began.

1. God asked Ezekiel whether he thought that the recovery of His covenant people, Israel, could really happen. Ezekiel answered, "You know" (Ezek. 37:3). Paul asked a similar question in 1 Corinthians 15:35 (AMPC): "But someone will say, How can the dead be raised? With what [kind of] body will they come forth?" Verse 36 warns that many things must die before they can come into the fullness of His plan.

So after God speaks to you, the first question is, "Can recovery happen?" Then the Lord says (as He said to Ezekiel), "Prophesy!" Warring with your prophetic word begins the moment you hear God's will and begin to prophesy it again.

2. Ezekiel prophesied exactly what God asked of him. This involved the declaring and shaping of the prophetic word. At the beginning of Ezekiel's prophesying, great movement occurred and bones reconnected. Yet we see in Ezekiel 37:8 that nothing was breathing. So, in verse 9, the Lord commanded him to prophesy again.

   I find that most of us quit the process as soon as movement seems to stop. But God wanted Ezekiel to prophesy until the breath returned. The second phase of warring with your prophetic word is to prophesy again.

3. Once the breath began, the dead condition of the bones had to be addressed. They were dried up; hope seemed lost; and the dead seemed cut off from the future. The real question was whether hope that was deferred could be restored.

   Then the Lord told Ezekiel to prophesy the opening of the graves! (See Ezekiel 37:12.) All the graveclothes of the dead—the things that held them captive—had to be removed. The graves would open and resurrected lives would return to the place of destiny, where God had planned for them to prosper.

   Often, you find yourself warring with death from a past season. A spirit of death must be broken for the Lord to continue His ultimate manifestation and will from heaven. This is phase three of warring with your prophetic word. Prophesy again!

4. The Lord then reminded Ezekiel to stop and look at the "whole," reiterating the original prophecy from Ezekiel 36 (which I previously recorded) in Ezekiel 37:14. He explained that what seemed hopelessly

scattered could return to God's original intent. An army could be resurrected and come together if Ezekiel continued to prophesy. Therefore, phase four of the process of prophecy is to prophesy *yet again*.

5. I love how the Lord repeats His intent of a new heart and a new spirit. The final phase of prophecy is to keep prophesying until you see the manifestation. Ask the Lord to give you strength to keep pressing forward until you see the performance of His Word. He will continue encouraging and helping you to know that He, the Lord, has spoken—the performance will come.

The message of warring is clear: Keep prophesying until you see what God has already spoken!

THERE WILL BE A MANIFESTATION

Remember, God has already given you a portion in life—a share in the abundance He has planned for you. As John 10:10 (AMP) declares, "The thief comes only in order to steal and kill and destroy. I came that they may have and enjoy life, and have it in abundance [to the full, till it overflows]." Hell despises the fact that God knew you before the foundation of the world and planned for great blessings to manifest along your path. However, the enemy cannot stop you unless you allow him access.

Jesus is faithful, reliable, and unchanging. He wants you to see in the end all that He has planned from the beginning. He intends for your latter days to surpass the former, and He desires for you to enjoy each day. Satan will seek to rob your joy through temptations, doubt, unbelief, and failures. He will use enemies and distractions to draw you away from God's purposes. Ultimately, your adversary is after your hope—your confident expectation that God's will shall be established in your life.

God has placed a bag of seeds in your hand to sow along your path. When you plant and nurture these seeds, they grow and produce wonderful fruit containing even more seeds, ensuring your future portion. You might lose some battles for your portion, but God's promise is that you can win the war. That means you must release past losses and continue to long for abundant life. (See Proverbs 13:12.) Remember, even in your Valley of Achor, God sets before you a door of hope—a divine escape from every scheme of your adversary.

Remain aware and ready to see your door. Regularly evaluate your resources and consider where you are in God's process. With every step bless and strengthen what He has given you. Give generously into your future—steward what remains so you may keep doing exploits for His kingdom.

Fix your gaze on hope. Hope is more than a wish; it is a trust-filled expectation that springs from the desires of your soul and anticipates what you do not yet see. If you want to see your God-given hopes fulfilled, keep watching. Hope does not produce guaranteed certainty, but neither does it disappoint. (See Romans 5:5.) Continue watching expectantly; press forward into your future—and what you desire will appear.

Recall that hope is not passive; it requires action, fresh goals, and purposeful movement along God's path. Hope creates optimism and enables you to overcome fears birthed by negative thoughts. You *need* hope. Stop and reflect where you are in your hope process. Then move to the offensive: Identify every way the enemy is working to steal your hope from you, and war on!

PROPHESY AGAINST ANY VOICE OF HOPELESSNESS

If you are human, you will at some point hear the voice of hopelessness during your lifetime. At certain times hope will overflow; at other times it will seem delayed or absent. Either way, hold on to every word God has spoken to you and consider the Lord's counsel to Ezekiel:

> Son of man, you've heard that proverb they quote in Israel:
> "Time passes, and prophecies come to nothing." Tell the
> people, "This is what the Sovereign LORD says: I will put an
> end to this proverb, and you will soon stop quoting it." Now
> give them this new proverb to replace the old one: "The time
> has come for every prophecy to be fulfilled!"
> —EZEKIEL 12:22–23, NLT

Proverbs 13:12 says, "Hope deferred makes the heart sick." When hope is delayed, the mind becomes uneasy, the heart sinks and threatens to fail, and we can become dispirited or even despondent. When we truly believe that all hope is lost, we simply give up on enjoying the blessings God has intended for us. But delayed hope can also have an opposite effect: It can challenge us to gain new vision!

I previously shared how the Lord led my wife and me to follow Him. This connected me to an organization that helped the USSR satellite countries connect with Mother Russia. The Lord visited me on December 31, 1983, and revealed exactly when He would open a window for the church to arise in those nations. He provided great detail, nation by nation, and revealed ways to prepare those nations for all that would come at the end of the 1980s. Never before had I encountered an angelic presence that communicated global events to me in such minute detail.

After that encounter the Lord led us sovereignly and shared with me that the USSR leader, Yuri Andropov, would die in 1984. Andropov passed away as the Lord said he would and was replaced by Konstantin Chernenko. The Lord had also clearly revealed that Andropov's replacement would be succeeded by yet another leader, and that person would hold office during the window of transformation that would open for the Soviet Bloc. I communicated these details to the leadership over me, and over the next five years, they prepared the church to rise in those nations.

To this day I am amazed that God chose me to participate in these events. By 1986 I was working with an organization focused on the Soviet Bloc nations. By June 4, 1989, communism was dismantled in Poland. On December 16, 1989, the Romanian revolution began, ultimately ending communist rule in that nation. On December 26, 1989, the Soviet Union was dissolved. Like dominoes, nations began to change!

ENTERING THE FUTURE WAR OF THE CHURCH

In 1986 I received another vision, where the Lord revealed events of the following forty years in ten-year increments. Much of what He showed me revolved around the church and a change in His kingdom's development. However, the nation He emphasized was China.

The 1986 vision revealed how China would rise to power. As I understood it, China would have a greater influence by 2006, and the eyes of the world would start turning in its direction. God showed me that, by 2016, China could be the most financially influential nation in the world. By 2026 they could rule the world. Russia would then align with China for a season and submit to its leading. America would have to resist with great effort or end up looking like China in the level of controls it exerts over its citizens in the days ahead.

At that time in the American church, anti-war sentiment was evident in the thoughts, actions, and prayers of God's people. When I shared this vision regarding China, it stirred controversy, and by the year 2000, the church's resistance to warfare increased.

Let me explain what God showed me back in 1986—what I was praying and contending to see happen—and some of the events that occurred:

1. 1986—This year marked a turning point for China, with student intellectuals calling for change, and the beginning of political and social reforms within the government. Student revolutions also arose to resist government oppression, which was evident throughout the nation—including within the Chinese church, which had long been pressured and controlled by the Communist government. I paid close attention

to these developments, having established relationships with five key leaders of the massive underground church.

2. **1989**—The student protest movement culminated in the Tiananmen Square protests (April 15 through June 4), which resulted in a massacre that awakened the world to China's extreme control.

3. **1996**—The Chinese government appeared more open to the world. Yet, even as certain reforms continued, some controls remained firmly in place.[2] I sensed that the government of the church needed to arise in a new way. An apostolic awareness would enter the earth, and new leadership would seek a shift from past church structures to a new kingdom movement.

   This was the year Peter Wagner convened the National Symposium on the Postdenominational Church at Fuller Seminary.[3] Bishop Bill Hamon regards it as a historical turning point for public recognition of the new apostolic movement.[4] The church in China, with its remarkable leadership, would become an integral part of this move. Since that time, the movement has swept the world.

4. **2006**—China increasingly entered the global picture, demonstrating economic strength and actively participating in the global community.[5] This activity aligned with China's desire to claim its presumed rightful place as a national power worldwide.

5. **2008**—The World Olympics in Beijing symbolized "China's ascension as a prosperous modern country and a great power."[6] Such an event would have seemed unimaginable twenty years earlier.

6. **2016**—By Rosh Hashanah 2016 (September/October), China sought to establish itself as the most influential nation in the world economy, pursuing a developmental strategy to make its economy second to none. At this point, the United States began to realign itself with China,[7] which would ultimately prove dangerous. Conflicts arose, and by 2018, the two nations began to distance themselves from a more cooperative relationship.[8]

7. **2020**—China made its most significant effort to gain world economic authority and bring nations under economic subjection, seemingly by any means possible. When COVID-19 first made headlines in 2019 from Wuhan—China's eighth-largest city by population and a prominent research center in Asia—I recognized the need to watch China very closely. I sensed this novel virus would not only affect China but sweep the globe. I also sensed that the virus would be a pawn in the world's economic chess match.

8. **2026**—By 2026 the goal of national China was to become the most dominant and controlling economic force in the world. The Lord showed me that an intervention in the 2024 election would be necessary to keep America from becoming subservient to China's economic rule.

As seen throughout these years, God was preparing me—and the rest of the church—for the future. The precision with which He did so was remarkable. Curiously, God revealed only ten-year increments up to 2026; I do not know why the vision stopped there, but that is the nature of revelation. One sees only what He is ready to reveal.

For example, the Lord showed me in January 1986 (technically, the day before) that the government of God would start changing by the end of January 1996. Then He revealed that, by the end of 2006, the church government would be in a new, mature state. This meant that a new wineskin would operate, and the way church had been operated from 1966 to 2006 would come to an end. I could document page after page of changes from various authors, but anyone who reads this book will know we are living in a different church era—one that Peter Wagner called the "New Apostolic Reformation."

The Lord showed me that, by 2006, lawlessness would find many avenues of operation throughout the world, which we have witnessed. He also revealed that, by 2016, many laws would be established to control the chaos, but those measures would severely restrict our freedom.

I also received advance understanding of what I call the "Sheep and Goat Nation Division," in which certain nations would align with the Lord, while other nations would oppose Him. The Lord showed me that a great change would occur in Russia by 2007, and the Russians would redevelop their plan of world domination. At the time I had a solid understanding of the former Soviet Bloc countries, owing to my work there throughout the 1980s. Yet I saw that they would have to realign with other nations this time, primarily in the Middle East.

Then the Lord gave me insight into England and showed me how the one-time driving force of the world would be "bought" by other nations, due to its own compromise. He indicated there would be a manifestation of this by 2016. But I must reiterate my belief that any of these negative outcomes can be changed by prayer.

God does not reveal such details to His people in order to cause dread or resignation. He reveals them so His church will be prepared to be the church in every circumstance. In all that He showed me, the nation He detailed most thoroughly was China, and His emphasis is undeniably significant. Of course, the United States was also on my mind, so I asked Him again, on May 31, 2008, "How will America survive in the days ahead?"

Of course, I continue to seek revelation on how to persist in prayer for the future. Because, whether we pay attention or not, the future is coming.

CHAPTER 8

THE VISION AND CALL TO AMERICA: WE NEED HEAVEN'S ASSISTANCE

As we pray and prophesy, God's vision becomes increasingly tangible. Obviously, the idea of God revealing something yet to come is not new. He has called many of His people to watch for what is ahead. It is a matter not only of watching but of planning and pursuing set goals according to what He has revealed, so that the vision becomes reality.

The prophet Habakkuk had firsthand experience with this process:

> Then the LORD answered me and said, "Write the vision and engrave it plainly on [clay] tablets so that the one who reads it will run.
> "For the vision is yet for the appointed [future] time it hurries toward the goal [of fulfillment]; it will not fail. Even though it delays, wait [patiently] for it, because it will certainly come; it will not delay."
>
> —HABAKKUK 2:2–3, AMP

The writer of the Book of Hebrews explains the process in this way:

FOR YET IN A VERY LITTLE WHILE, HE WHO IS COMING WILL COME, AND WILL NOT DELAY. BUT MY RIGHTEOUS ONE [the one justified by faith] SHALL LIVE BY FAITH [respecting man's relationship to God and trusting Him]; AND IF HE DRAWS BACK [shrinking in fear], MY SOUL HAS NO DELIGHT IN HIM.

But our way is not that of those who shrink back to destruction, but [we are] of those who believe [relying on God through faith in Jesus Christ, the Messiah] and by this confident faith preserve the soul.

—HEBREWS 10:37–39, AMP

Prophetic workings are essential to the church, which is called to affect the world. I am called to the nations, and now you understand more about how I have focused on that call. At the same time my own country is part of God's plans. Therefore, He has called me to pray for America.

GO TO ALL THE STATES

At the end of 2002, as I flew into Washington, DC, to attend some meetings, the Lord impressed me with these words: "For this nation to change, I need you to visit every state and rally My army." This was a stretching moment in my life: I already had many commitments. I spoke and traveled all over the world. I had a large family, led a vibrant church, and served on many ministry boards. Therefore, I knew the Lord would have to fully confirm this assignment to me.

Soon the Lord orchestrated some peculiar events. Dutch Sheets met me in DC for ministry and leadership gatherings, and he asked me this question: "What do you hear the Lord saying?" So I told him what I told you about traveling to every state in our nation. With a peculiar look on his face, he said, "The Lord has spoken the same thing to me!"

Our lives were about to change. We had the promise from God that if we would go, the nation we love would also change. So, over the next two years, we aligned our apostolic and prophetic gifts, traveling to all fifty US states on what we called the Fifty-State Tour.

People from across each state attended our meetings. We shared what God was doing in the body of Christ and in our nation. Then we prophesied to each state. Dutch would discuss realignment, focusing especially on how God was restoring order and teaching about the concept of time.

Dutch's favorite scripture about time was from Isaiah 46:10: "Declaring the end from the beginning, and from ancient times things that are not yet done, saying, 'My counsel shall stand, and I will do all My pleasure.'" Another translation of the verse's second part (NASB) says, "My plan will be established, and I will accomplish all My good pleasure." Dutch always tied this verse to Job 22:28 (NASB), which says, "You will also decide something, and it will be established for you; and light will shine on your ways." Dutch understood Job's point to mean that if God reveals something He declared in the past, you can decree it into a different time frame. When you do, light will emerge and illuminate your path in that season.

Together, Dutch and I wrote a prophetic history book called *Releasing the Prophetic Destiny of a Nation.*[1] In 2024 Destiny Image updated the book, adding two more chapters by Tim Sheets. It's all about pressing forward for America. If you don't have the book, I believe it'll be an essential addition to your library.

ANGELIC VISITATION IS NECESSARY

I firmly believe we have entered a harvest season. In December 2017 the Lord chose me for an angelic visitation. He caught me up and showed me His scythe sweeping across the heavens and setting the nations into a new alignment.

As He moved His scythe, two developments unfolded. First, demonic powers holding people captive in the earth realm tightened their grip. Yet the Lord said, "But I have harvesters whom I am preparing to send forth." He revealed His plan to train these harvesters and send them into the fields of the nations. Second, I witnessed nations themselves realigning for harvest. God has a government; He is Lord Sabaoth, the God of hosts—commander of the armies of heaven. He orchestrates the hosts of heaven to work in concert with His kingdom army on earth. When we walk in His glory, angelic visitation takes place, and as His earthly army, we must partner with the heavenly hosts. Through this partnership God's victory is released in our earthly realm.

During that visitation I saw an angel intently observing the harvest across the earth. When I asked his name, he answered, "I am the Angel of War over God's Covenant Harvest Plan."

Next, the angel revealed the shift that awaits the harvesters and announced it was time to break out of conventional ways of thinking. I realized we must embrace this shift and move through the gate of harvest increase. There will be a great hardening, followed by separation and then sharpening, which will call forth the army order within the body of Christ. This was the *first harvest training*!

The Angel of War then guided me through additional training steps that will be fulfilled in the future:

- Grace will be sovereignly extended for past covenant misalignments. This becomes the *second harvest training*, addressing the Hagars, Ishmaels, and Esaus in our lives—as well as any brothers or sisters who have persecuted us.

- The eyes of the saints will be opened to the carrion scavengers that have ravished their covenant plan. This is the *third harvest training* (focusing on bloodline and mission).

- New angelic councils will be formed and assigned to territories. These teams will convene with apostolic-prophetic councils in the earth realm, providing strategies for advancement. This is the *fourth harvest training*.

- The "desire of nations" (Jesus) will begin to reveal Himself! Civil leaders will issue public decrees, calling entire territories and peoples into awakening. This is the *fifth harvest training*.

- God's people will be sorted according to their faithfulness to gather and steward what remains. This faithfulness will allow them to move from gleaning to reaping and will mark the *sixth harvest training.*

- The territorial threshing floors for the harvest will be revealed, and new calls will be issued to harvesters. This is the *seventh harvest training.*

As the God of hosts, the Lord brings angels and saints together to advance His kingdom. I believe we are now in a season of heightened angelic visitation. Already, we are likely visited by more angels than we realize. In *The New Era of Glory: Stepping Into God's Accelerated Season of Outpouring and Breakthrough,* apostle Tim Sheets describes the coming glory war and offers a road map for the days ahead.[2] His book moves us beyond our present understanding and into revelation for a new era. Notice what the following passage describes:

> After these things I looked, and behold, a door standing open in heaven. And the first voice which I heard was like a trumpet speaking with me, saying, "Come up here, and I will show you things which must take place after this." Immediately I was in the Spirit; and behold, a throne set in heaven, and One sat on the throne.
>
> —REVELATION 4:1–2

God is opening a door in the heavenly realm and aligning it over us in the earthly realm. This door provides angelic help and opens the way to our future. This is exactly what I believe we are experiencing: Heavenly portals are being opened, and God's angelic host is flooding into our atmosphere.

The Spirit of God is saying, "Go forth by My Spirit with My help, with My ministering angelic host, and do the war ahead." In the season we have entered, we need angelic interaction like never before. We must understand their visitation once the portal of glory has connected heaven and earth.

I have seen angels only a few times, but I do recognize their presence. I believe this discernment comes through worship and by recognizing the glory of God and the way His presence manifests around us. Imagine the angels appearing to announce in the fields near Bethlehem that the glory of God had come to earth!

Yes, angels often precede God's glory, but they also follow after it.[3]

GOD'S TRIUMPHANT RESERVE

As I stated in the previous chapter, I had to ask the Lord again in 2008, "How will America survive in the days ahead?" From September 2007 through that fall, winter, and even part of the spring of 2008, I continued to minister as the Lord led me. I love ministering to God's people. We are a peculiar, precious people in this world. However, on May 31, 2008, an event occurred that has changed my life to this day.

At the time John and Sheryl Price, Peter and Trisha Roselle, and the state leadership of New Jersey invited me to Liberty State Park to "Open the Gates in 2008" so that the glory of God might flood across America. Liberty State Park is located on the American mainland in New Jersey, directly across from Ellis Island. Historically, many who settled the East Coast—and much of the United States—first arrived on Ellis Island, declared their desire to be part of this nation, and then traveled by ferry to other New York City locales or to the train terminal in Jersey City to reach other destinations.[4]

The leadership team that invited me to speak rented the train station at Liberty State Park for a worship gathering. Before the regional meeting started, I could feel the Spirit of God moving on me. When worship began, the Spirit of God fell on me, and I was caught up into a heavenly place. In that moment I received a vision in which the Lord lifted me and showed me the US. First, I saw His remnant and where they were positioned. Next, He showed me their strength, from state to state to state.

I asked, "Lord, what are You showing me?"

It was as if a magnet was drawing the troops. They gathered

from every part of each state, forming what appeared to be a river of glory fire. I asked, "Lord, who are these people?"

He answered, "This is My Triumphant Reserve for the future!"

A vision unfolded of the reserve He would call for His future kingdom purposes. Many departed from the enemy's camp of religion, while others chose to remain within familiar religious structures. As God assembled this new reserve, large groups felt unmoved by the movement, and some aligned themselves based on race or gender rather than mission or calling. Nevertheless, He indicated how this fiery river of God's people would ultimately destroy the works of the enemy.

A new scene emerged: High places, established through years of idolatrous worship and wrongful sacrifice, stood in every American state. These were worship altars, constructed as strategic footholds by the enemy. Sacrifices on these altars, I saw, empowered ruling enemy hosts to keep atmospheres captive.

The focus shifted to the atmosphere itself—its layers in relation to God's presence and the contrast with demonic spiritual rule pervading certain regions. In some areas darkness had already prevailed. Ten enemy-developed ruling centers within the US functioned as communication hubs, transmitting to lesser substations across the nation. I observed how sacrifices empowered evil presences, which then communicated between centers, each network supporting a larger plan of control.

Attention moved to the nation's covenant roots and the nurturing of those grafted into God's promise, a legacy back to Abraham's obedience. Although initially sustained by this covenant root, many lifelines had since withered. In some regions roots were covered by a mossy, evil slime that could yet be removed; in others the land had never permitted a covenant root to grow. Broken covenants, I realized, would need mending before fruitfulness could return.

Later, conflicts among the root systems became apparent—conflicts that would determine the sort of fruit brought forth in the coming years. These tensions, I discerned, would multiply and intensify. Soon orchards of contention began to emerge in the vision. Interestingly, each orchard's people groups yielded unfamiliar fruit. The only biblical parallel that came to mind was the church at Antioch—an international church established for kingdom advancement during a unique season in history.

Additional revelation concerned how the US communication system was intertwined internationally, while a new form of global communications was taking root in the demonic world. Such systems would influence financial and legal structures, establishing a dominant voice set in opposition to the God of Israel. On that basis I understood that the next seven years, beginning in 2008, would bring much warfare for Israel.

Yet not all revelation was foreboding. I witnessed remnant buildings taking shape—fiery, vibrant castles strategically placed throughout the earth. Not every state had one, but when I asked the Lord what they were, He answered, "These are My freedom outposts for the future." It was clear His Triumphant Reserve would connect with these centers; those entering would depart seven times brighter and stronger.

I was shown twenty-one states with deep covenant roots, while two others—Florida and California—hung in the balance. Many conservative-minded people write off California, viewing the state as so left-wing that the nation would be better off without it. But God's perspective on California is different.

From heaven I could see two ruling root structures contending for California's future: an evil root of humanism, empowered by leftist ideology, and a glory root called Awakening. The outcome of this struggle would not only shape the West Coast but also significantly affect America as a whole.

Many states had freedom outposts. (I now realize that these are the apostolic centers the Lord will form as gathering places for His Triumphant Reserve. Robert Heidler and I explain this point in a previously referenced book.) In other regions additional outposts would need to form in some places—especially where the spiritual atmosphere remained resistant to freedom. New forms of warfare would become necessary for His triumphant people to reclaim portions of the land.

During this four-hour visitation, the Lord revealed that prayer strategies from the previous season would no longer be effective. Nazareth and Capernaum are good examples of this in Jesus' day. Neither city recognized their hour of visitation and rejected the new wineskin Jesus offered them. I thought of how the Lord told the disciples, "This kind does not go out except by prayer and fasting" (Matt. 17:21), which was another call to shift into a new season. He showed me how His Triumphant Reserve would enter a dimension of worship and war that He had reserved for the time ahead.

> **GOD'S NEW LEADERSHIP COMES NOT ONLY FROM THE YOUNG BUT FROM REALIGNED GENERATIONS.**

The vision from 2008 continued with 153 nations that would align with Israel and become sheep nations for the future. Since the massacre by Hamas on October 7, 2023, I have watched nations choose their corners. Nations that desire to embrace the following prophetic word from the Book of Zechariah will also choose to align and become God's sheep nations:

> Then everyone who is left of all the nations that went against Jerusalem will go up from year to year to worship the King, the LORD of hosts, and celebrate the Feast of Booths (Tabernacles). And it will be that whichever of the families of the earth does not go up to Jerusalem to worship the King, the LORD of hosts, there will be no rain on them.
>
> —ZECHARIAH 14:16–17, AMP

Fresh calls delivered by angels are now being released from heaven into the earth. Through today's intercession and travail, the gates of heaven are opening for these calls to come to those equipped to lead in this critical hour. God's new leadership comes not only from the young but from realigned generations. It is as though a multigenerational army, like David's, is being picked for this moment in history. When they align, their hearts become one with His, and His strength is released for victory.

AMERICA WILL HAVE TO PLAY THE TRUMP CARD

In the visitation on May 31, 2008, the Lord answered the question I had asked Him about how America would survive in the days ahead. He told me, "America can change by learning to play the Trump card"; afterward, He revealed how a Triumphant Reserve would arise. In my book *Redeeming the Time*, I first wrote about this encounter and what triumph would mean in the days ahead.[5] I wrote, "An easy way to understand triumph is to think of a card played that takes all others (as in *trumping* and winning a hand or suit)."[6]

I also shared this vision in *The Apostolic Church Arising* and *A Time to Triumph*.[7] In this latest book, I wrote,

> God has a Kingdom of people, a nation above all nations. These people hold the "trump card" of influence over the world, the flesh and the devil—*oh my*! Built within God's children is His covenant authority to be used in a timely manner. When we exercise God's authority within us, we will overtake every plan of the enemy and release a strategy of fullness in the earth.[8]

Somehow, I recognized in 2008 that Donald Trump had been chosen by the Lord to become a US president. I don't believe that elections are about a person; in my view they are about changing a nation. I saw even then that God had begun to fully define the course for America. However, we would have to learn to play the "Trump card."

I DON'T BELIEVE THAT ELECTIONS ARE ABOUT A PERSON; IN MY VIEW THEY ARE ABOUT CHANGING A NATION.

Donald Trump is an interesting, bold, and abrasive person, so I wondered how the Lord would develop the "Trump card." I had prophesied in 2005 that the next president in America would be African American. Barack Obama came on the scene, and the Lord fulfilled this prophecy. Now God seemed to be presenting Donald Trump as a card Americans would have to play. Anyone who knows me knows that I am not a card sharp. But I know that, in card playing, there is a card that no one can beat. The question was how America would get this card.

The answer came in 2016, when Donald Trump defeated Hillary Clinton and became the forty-fifth US president. Oh my! Lots of changes and much resistance soon enveloped America. Steve Strang has written several books about the presidency of Donald Trump and all that transpired as a result. His books—*God and Donald Trump*, *Trump Aftershock*, and *God, Trump and the 2020 Election* explain more about the significance of President Donald Trump.[9]

Looking back, a certain detail from the May 31, 2008, visitation seems perhaps even more interesting than it did at the time: The Spirit of the Lord revealed that President Trump would have only three and a half years to influence and change the nation before being removed for a time. The Lord gave me a scripture passage related to this:

> Then He began telling them this parable: "A certain man had a fig tree that had been planted in his vineyard; and he came looking for fruit on it, but did not find any; so he said to the vineyard-keeper, 'For three years I have come looking for fruit on this fig tree and have found none. Cut it down! Why does it even use up the ground [depleting the soil and blocking the sunlight]?' But he replied to him, 'Let it alone, sir, [just] one more year until I dig around it and put in fertilizer; and if it bears fruit after this, fine; but if not, cut it down.'"
>
> —LUKE 13:6–9, AMP

The Lord impressed upon me in the fourth year of President Trump's first term that He would determine whether America would be a righteous nation in the future. To do this He would remove Donald Trump for a season—allowing America to truly see what she had become. In November 2020, Joe Biden was elected president with much controversy. The nation was already enduring great conflict through the COVID-19 pandemic, a new uprising of "woke" mentality, and the development of liberal the-ology—all in a dark attempt to make the America of 2026 look like what I had seen in 1986.

But God! Glory always has the final say.

Meanwhile, Dutch Sheets continued to visit states and rally a remnant in prayer without me. Since our fifty-state tour, I have probably visited every state three or more times for prophetic apostolic meetings. Following the upheaval of the 2020 election and the futile attempts to overturn it, I held on to what God said. He would dig around in America to see whether the nation would produce fruit in the days ahead.

THE BARGE DREAM AND REVERSE IMAGING

On May 6, 2020, as *The Passover Prophecies* was ready to go to press, I had a dream and felt compelled to share it in that book. In the dream I was steering a shipping barge to its new position in a port. It was the first barge that I had ever helped dock, and I did a satisfactory job. (I believe this first ship represented the ways in which God led our team to facilitate intercessory prayer efforts during President Trump's first term in office.)

Suddenly, the timing of the dream changed, and I was required to dock a second barge in a different port. This docking job was much trickier than the first, but I instantly knew how to guide the barge into port: I would use mirrors, as I did for the first docking, but in a new way. During the first docking, I had misin-terpreted several reflections, which caused me problems. Now, on the mirrors I was using, I saw crucial reflections of other nations that were trading in the port. To get the boat into position, I had to maneuver around and past these nations. Once I understood what they were trading, I used that knowledge to guide the barge into place.

One challenge was getting the barge through a narrow entryway that was only half as wide as the barge. On each side of the vessel were other barges from Russia and China. Guiding *my* barge into port required greater mastery of the mirrors that were available to me—mirrors that I could attach to the barge. These mirrors would produce reverse imaging that would allow me to park successfully.

In my dream there was no way to maneuver the barge through the port to its docking position without the use of mirrors. But mirror images are reversed, and unless you interpret the images correctly, you will impede your vessel's movement. This is true in life and in decoding the symbolic information and revelation that comes through dreams. Before sharing the rest of the dream, let me dig a little deeper into reverse images.[10]

—m—

Because I believe this idea is important to understanding the dream, I asked Lisa Lyons, a Global Spheres Center staffer, to research reverse imaging. Here's what she learned: Reverse imaging processes image information to produce a picture or trace an original picture's origin. It is similar to the process of criminal forensics, in which elements of a crime scene are analyzed to re-create or explain the what/when/how/who/why of events. You work backward from the end result until the end reveals the beginning.

This principle is pervasive throughout God's ways, allowing us to embrace the cyclical truths of His reality within our natural lives. All the time processes at work in the creation move in cycles—evening to morning to evening, first day to seventh day to first day again, month's beginning to month's end to month's beginning, and so forth for the years themselves. Time rolls over on itself, and every time we come to an end, we are at a beginning again. Such is the essence of reverse imaging.

Reverse imaging should be operating within our revelatory process: When the Lord speaks, we either hear or see something. From that place we can search backward for the truths out of which the revelation sprang. This allows us to better understand what He is revealing now and how to move forward in it. Lisa wrote,

Chuck's dream of backing up a barge using mirrors speaks into this: He had to take the images present in the mirrors and process that information backward to see how to safely maneuver and park the barge. Chuck is a master "reverse imager" and it's part of the reason his prophetic gift is so prodigious; he doesn't just hear or see but is able to invert revelation and walk backward in it to capture all of what the Lord is saying…and then release it.[11]

When I awakened from the barge dream, I was under the impression that Donald Trump would have a second term. From that second term, we could work backward to find our place among the nations. I shared this with Steve Strang in 2020 as well as with others in 2022 when Mr. Trump decided to run for president again.

—⁓—

Returning to the dream: When I finally parked the barge, I realized that I needed to update Pam on my location and what I was doing. I reached for my cell phone but knew it was not the proper way to communicate. It's not that I physically couldn't use my cell phone—I just understood that using it would thwart the business that we had in the port. In other words, the line was not secure.

By this time I was in a lounge at the port, where I noticed a landline. I unplugged the phone and the line from the wall and brought them into a glass business-center setting. I tried to use the landline but couldn't get through and realized I needed a certain code to access an outside line. I thought I could figure out the code, but I also realized that the landline phone was not the right mode of communication either.

The barge captain came into the lounge and asked if I was trying to use the phone.

I said, "Yes."

He said, "Using the landline will cost you an exorbitant amount of money, and you need a code. Let me bring you another communication device."

I had the impression that the call might be traced to me because of the enormous bill that would have to be paid. Then the captain returned with a new, hidden device—an odd pay-phone-looking thing about the size of a watch box. I realized that activating the phone and making a successful connection would require the insertion of a coin from our current US-dollar-based economy into a portion of the device.

Once the device was activated, I could make my call using a money-clip-like wallet phone. But this portion of the device required some sort of new currency to complete the communication. This new currency was like cryptocurrency but was something else that I knew I didn't have. I realized that a chip in it would cause the device to work, and no other currency would do.

That was where the dream ended.[12]

Here are several key insights I believe the 2020 dream revealed:

- US trade systems would be severely tested. In the days ahead, these systems will become established in current and new ports by new means. The coming season of trade will be much more difficult than the past.

- The US would have to realign with key nations. These were the nations I saw reflected in the mirrors I used to maneuver the second barge into the port. (This included Spain, Italy, Argentina, Brazil, Mexico, Morocco, Saudi Arabia, Great Britain, and Germany, to name a few.) These nations had already established themselves in the port.

- The US would have to contend with China. In my dream I knew China was in control of the port's overall operations. As I interpreted it, we would see growing contention with China over dominance in world trade.

- The US communication system would have to change as quickly as possible. One of China's ongoing "war tactics" (in terms of trade, economics, and world power) will be to lock us out of certain trade ports. Our only way of becoming established may be by maneuvering through other nations and using a different kind of communication system.

- Somehow, gold would be key to the new currency.

- There would be a second term for President Trump. In my dream I believe the second port represented Donald Trump's second term in office. Although I published this dream in *The Passover Prophecies* in 2020, I hadn't clearly heard from the Holy Spirit whether President Trump would be reelected. But this dream was my first inkling in the Spirit of a possible second term.

- Churches and nations would have to operate differently. As mentioned earlier, the ways in which the church and the nation operated in the past season would not suffice in the new one. We must let go of the old—so too must President Trump. To be successful in his second term, he must grasp principles that were not interpreted correctly in his first.[13]

The way the Lord emphasized China to me in 1986 remains telling today. I knew in 2020 and beyond that if Trump didn't return to office, China would become the dominant world power in terms of trade and economics—an unjoyful prospect for the world and for freedom.

ISRAEL IS THE KEY

Something else happened on May 6, 2020: Israel's Supreme Court ruled that Prime Minister Benjamin Netanyahu could form a new government. This "ended a 17-month political stalemate and prevented the country from plunging into a fourth consecutive election in just over a year."[14]

We must realign with Israel for trade. When Israel was coming of age as a modern nation, many other nations resisted trading and working with it. The Israelis had to learn creatively how to grow, produce, and use their own food. They had to develop many innovative products and systems. We will see similar needs for communication in the future, and Israel will help develop ways for us to communicate so our trade system will flourish.

Remember, on October 7, 2023, Hamas breached the borders aligned with Gaza and massacred nearly 1,200 people, including Israelis and foreign nationals. This was the greatest loss of Jewish life at one time since the Holocaust. Israel responded by going to war with Hamas. This exposed the real war assignment that Iran pursued through Hezbollah in Syria and Lebanon. From my perspective their goal was to take Israel out of God's timing for the sovereign revelation of His covenant power to the world.

The October 7 massacre and the resulting war in the Middle East caused the nations to awaken to Israel. However, these events also created a global dichotomy—a fresh line of demarcation between those who will align with Israel and those who will not.

A SEASON OF ACCELERATED HARVEST

The Lord has prepared to extend my call to America in a new way. When He visited me at Liberty Park in 2008, He disclosed that everything He revealed would begin to happen by 2020. Later, in 2020, He impressed on me that the harvest of His kingdom would accelerate in America by 2024. However, I was unsure of my role in this call to harvest—or, at least, I was until 2022.

On August 10, 2022, Dutch Sheets and I ministered during a meeting at The Citadel in South Carolina, one of America's senior public war colleges, which also holds worship services. During worship the Lord caught me up and gave me a vision of four key war angels positioned to the north, south, east, and west of America.

Soon afterward, I saw fifty-one angels encircle this nation, and I heard the Lord say, "I am getting ready to commission change."

All the angels had their swords sheathed, so they were not ready to be sent for war *yet*. However, each one would be assigned to a particular state, and each state would face divine choices. Ultimately, each angel would harvest its assigned state based upon the choices that state had made in sowing and alignment during the past season.

The four key angels, plus fifty-one angels assigned to the states

I want to encourage you that, because of our prayers, America is now surrounded by a supernatural angelic force. The Lord revealed to me that in April 2024, things would start changing rapidly. If a state does not resolidify its covenant with the Lord, judgments will begin to come to that state. We must remember that in God's time of harvest, we are harvested one way or the other, based upon what we have sown and the choices we have made.

Spiritual visitation is like an audit, in which a territorial angel evaluates a state's Triumphant Reserve and kingdom harvesters in relation to what the Overseer is seeking. This is part of what Yeshua's visitation was about in the latter portion of His earthly ministry, when He stated this warning:

As He approached Jerusalem, He saw the city and wept over it [and the spiritual ignorance of its people], saying, "If [only] you had known on this day [of salvation], even you, the things which make for peace [and on which peace depends]! But now they have been hidden from your eyes. For a time [of siege] is coming when your enemies will put up a barricade [with pointed stakes] against you, and surround you [with armies] and hem you in on every side, and they will level you to the ground, you [Jerusalem] and your children within you. They will not leave in you one stone on another, all because you did not [come progressively to] recognize [from observation and personal experience] the time of your visitation [when God was gracious toward you and offered you salvation]."

—LUKE 19:41–44, AMP

I know that when God calls me to America, He moves with apostolic and prophetic authority to create a new kingdom rule. Based on what the Lord revealed to me at The Citadel on August 10, 2022, harvesting in America began to change in April 2024, and He will make each state's position very clear.

> **IN GOD'S TIME OF HARVEST, WE ARE HARVESTED BASED UPON WHAT WE HAVE SOWN AND THE CHOICES WE HAVE MADE.**

The vision I received at The Citadel reminded me of Isaiah's visitation with the seraphim. The prophet Isaiah wrote, "In the year that King Uzziah died, I saw the Lord" (6:1). The seraphim caught Isaiah up and showed him a dimension of what would happen. (See Isaiah 6:2–13.) Verse 13 mentions a stump that would come alive. I believe the angels that are auditing the US states will find the stump in each state and attempt to bring life from it. If life does not come forth, I think residents will recognize that something is very wrong in their state. The reckoning will be visible, and there will be no confusion.

A testimony of grace will also develop in each state, serving as a staking of a claim for each state and territory. I also saw that, in April 2024, America would begin a refocus to include a change in

civil government and then a mobilization of the new remnant—
the aforementioned Triumphant Reserve.

THE GATE OF HARVEST IS OPENING

One of my main questions for the Lord on August 10, 2022,
involved how we would mobilize this new remnant for the coming
harvest season. I knew each state needed to gather; however, I also
saw the great changes that had occurred since March 2020, when
the COVID-19 pandemic was in its early stage. So I wondered how
this gathering would unfold.

Speaking personally, my airline travel miles had plunged from
my yearly pattern of 550,000 miles. We began to use Zoom to
communicate virtually and hosted numerous conferences from
our studio at the Global Spheres Center. I realized that we could
build a new virtual platform for the states, enabling each state and
its key leaders to rally online. We could record each meeting and
make the videos available to the entire nation.

That is exactly what we did—later called Surrounding the
Nation. (See https://tv.gloryofzion.org/surrounding-the-nation.)
The main reason for these meetings was to invite each state's territorial angel. Prophetic decrees would be initiated, allowing God's
plans for harvest to be heard and ultimately accomplished. We
also watched the placement of each angel's sword to see whether
it was still sheathed.

In addition to fifty-one online gatherings, we continued hosting
on-site gatherings coinciding with God's biblical timetable. We
also held virtual Shabbat services every Friday night and gathered at Firstfruits to present the blessings God had made available
to us as we continued moving forward in time. We hosted larger
gatherings for Passover, Pentecost, and the Feast of Tabernacles.
All three events were available virtually, but we also encouraged
people to come on-site at the Global Spheres Center, which houses
Glory of Zion International Ministries. I believe this apostolic
center has become a worldwide prototype of God's kingdom plan

for freedom outposts. (For a better visual understanding, please go to www.gloryofzion.org.)

WHERE DO I GO FROM HERE?

No matter where you are presently, you need to know that as long as you are still breathing, you have a path ahead. At every key moment in your life, ask, "Where do I go from here?" The same holds true for our nation; we need to ask God where we are headed.

Even as we pray and prophesy, we still depend on heaven's assistance. Thankfully, the Lord offers it! He wants His vision to become increasingly real to us. He is never confused or uncertain; He sees with perfect clarity. He knows our path, and He knows we have a future. But can we recognize the next step? Let's consider that question together.

CHAPTER 9

LORD, CAN YOU SHOW ME SOMETHING BEYOND 2026?

A s Jesus prepared His disciples for His departure, He said, "When the Spirit of truth comes, he will guide you into all truth. He will not speak on his own but will tell you what he has heard. He will tell you about the future. He will bring me glory by telling you whatever he receives from me" (John 16:13–14, NLT). Through decades of walking with the Lord, I have seen this passage play out in people's lives over and over again. Although we may not see as clearly as Jesus did, the Holy Spirit still reveals to us what He has heard.

During the election of 2024, people often asked me who would win. I was perplexed, because I had in mind what *should* happen, but I didn't have an assurance or a desire to publicly proclaim a definite outcome. That seemed to surprise some people, who said, "But you are a prophet—you know what will happen."

The night before the election, I simply asked the Lord, "Can You show me anything past 2026?" Then I fell asleep.

On November 5, 2024, at 3:14 a.m., the Lord awakened me and said, "Hezekiah—extend time!" So I began to ponder Hezekiah's life. I knew the good he did and the mistakes he made, but I was not sure what the Lord was getting at. At 4 a.m. I received a call from Israel. The caller said, "God is saying 'Hezekiah' to you."

That was more than a confirmation! I reread every biblical

passage related to Hezekiah. When I reached Isaiah 37, the Lord illuminated the following verses:

> This shall be the sign [of these things] to you [Hezekiah]: you are to eat this year what grows of itself, and in the second year that which springs from the same, and in the third year you are to sow and harvest, and plant vineyards and eat their fruit. The surviving remnant of the house of Judah will again take root downward and bear fruit upward. For out of Jerusalem will come a remnant and from Mount Zion a band of survivors. The zeal of the LORD of hosts will do this.
> —ISAIAH 37:30–32, AMP

I immediately stopped and said, "Lord, that is speaking of three years ahead." The first year would be 2025, the second would be 2026, and the third would be 2027—when the remnant would take root and bear fruit. I jumped and began to rejoice. The Lord had taken me beyond 2026!

HEZEKIAH, SENNACHERIB, RABSHAKEH, AND THE PROPHET

What God revealed was how the breaker anointing would take His people beyond 2026. The breaker anointing allows God's people to operate on levels of power and authority that go far beyond answered prayer, as when Jesus spoke with divine authority to break the enemy's power. Likewise, when someone is praying, facing obstacles, and it appears that nothing is happening, the breaker anointing takes that person past the clutter.

One of the most amazing descriptions of the breaker anointing is found in the story of Hezekiah and Sennacherib. (See 2 Kings 18 and 2 Chronicles 32.) Hezekiah loved God and was one of the godliest kings Judah ever had. One of his first acts as king was to cleanse and restore the temple. He then restored the celebration of Passover. (See 2 Chronicles 29:3–19; 30:1–27.) The people enjoyed it so much that they decided to have a double Passover celebration! (See 2 Chronicles 30:23.)

Hezekiah was a man of praise, whom many scholars credit with writing several psalms. He led the people into praise; Scripture reveals that "he stationed the Levites in the house of the LORD with cymbals, with stringed instruments, and with harps....The singers sang; and the trumpeters sounded....
The king and all who were present with him bowed and worshiped" (2 Chron. 29:25, 28, 29). Hezekiah instructed the Levites to praise the Lord, so they sang praises with gladness, bowed their heads, and worshipped. Like David, Hezekiah was a man after God's heart.

However, in 701 BC, Sennacherib, the king of Assyria, invaded Judah, conquered the major cities, and marched on Jerusalem.

> **SENNACHERIB DID TO HIS FOES WHAT SATAN DOES TO US— HE USED WORDS TO UNDERMINE THE JEWS' CONFIDENCE IN THEIR GOD.**

The Assyrians were known throughout the ancient world for their sadistic cruelty in torturing conquered peoples. Although their army was the most powerful in the world, Sennacherib seemed to prefer winning by intimidation. He therefore waged a campaign of terror against the people of Jerusalem. According to 2 Kings 18:17 (NIV), Sennacherib sent his supreme commander with a large army to deliver a chilling message. It began with these words: "This is what the great king, the king of Assyria, says."

SENNACHERIB'S INTIMIDATION

Sennacherib did to his foes what Satan does to us—he used words to undermine the Jews' confidence in their God. Satan and his emissaries love to tell us, "God won't really save you." Then they paint horrible pictures in our minds, showing how we will suffer when God lets us down.

This is exactly what Sennacherib did. He goaded his foes by saying, "When Hezekiah says, 'The LORD our God will save us from the hand of the king of Assyria,' he is misleading you, to let you die of hunger and thirst" (2 Chron. 32:11, NIV). The Assyrian king persisted and said, "Do you not know what I and

my predecessors have done to all the peoples of the other lands?...
Just as [their gods] did not rescue their people from my hand,
so the god of Hezekiah will not rescue [you] from my hand"
(vv. 13, 17, NIV).

Just as Satan offers God's people bad bargains and accuses
God of not caring for them, Sennacherib's messenger offered
God's people a deal, saying, "Come now, make a bargain with my
master" (2 Kings 18:23, NIV). He also accused the Lord, saying,
"Furthermore, have I come to attack and destroy this place without
word from the LORD? The LORD himself told me to march against
this country and destroy it" (v. 25, NIV).

Later in 2 Chronicles 32:18 (NIV), we read that Sennacherib's
officers "called out in Hebrew to the people of Jerusalem who
were on the wall, to terrify them and make them afraid in order
to capture the city." Sennacherib followed Satan's primary strategy,
which was to terrify people, knowing that if he succeeded, he
would take them captive.

Lastly, Sennacherib tried a different approach. He said, "Make
peace with me and come out to me. Then each of you will eat
fruit from your own vine and fig tree and drink water from your
own cistern, until I come and take you to a land like your own—a
land of grain and new wine, a land of bread and vineyards, a land
of olive trees and honey" (2 Kings 18:31–32, NIV). He borrowed
Satan's ploy, essentially saying, "You think I'm a monster, but I'm
really Santa Claus. Come out and trust me."

HEZEKIAH'S RESPONSE

When the enemy surrounded the city and shouted his threats,
Hezekiah knew exactly what to do: He sought the Lord. Second
Kings 19:1 (NIV) says, "When King Hezekiah heard this, he tore
his clothes and put on sackcloth and went into the temple of the
LORD." He not only prayed but also sent a message to the prophet
Isaiah and asked him to pray too.

So Hezekiah and Isaiah prayed fervently, but the enemy
remained outside the gate. It appeared that their prayers had

changed nothing, until Isaiah received and uttered this prophetic word from the Lord: "Do not be afraid of what you have heard.... Listen! When he hears a certain report, I will make him want to return to his own country, and there I will have him cut down with the sword" (Isa. 37:6–7, NIV).

Still nothing changed! In 2 Kings 19 Sennacherib sent more messengers to Hezekiah, this time with a letter, saying, "Do not let the god you depend on deceive you when he says, 'Jerusalem will not be given into the hands of the king of Assyria.' Surely you have heard what the kings of Assyria have done to all the countries, destroying them completely. And will you be delivered?" (vv. 10–11, NIV).

We've all been there. You pray hard and receive an encouraging prophetic word, yet the situation stagnates and the enemy continues his threats. Hezekiah trusted God but remained under pressure. He knew that if the Assyrians took Jerusalem, he and his family would be tortured to death, and the city he loved would be destroyed. He could see the strength of Sennacherib's armies, and the situation continued to look hopeless.

So what did Hezekiah do? He took Sennacherib's letter up to the temple. There, he "spread [the letter] out before the LORD. And Hezekiah prayed to the LORD" (vv. 14–15, NIV). The king essentially said, "Lord, look at what the enemy is saying—he is ridiculing You!" (See 2 Kings 19:16.)

Then, in the midst of what seemed like a lost cause, Hezekiah turned his heart to the Lord in praise. He "prayed before the LORD, and said: 'O LORD God of Israel, the One who dwells between the cherubim, You are God, You alone, of all the kingdoms of the earth. You have made heaven and earth'" (v. 15).

As Hezekiah praised God, everything shifted. God spoke to Isaiah again—this time releasing the breaker anointing. Isaiah's new word included this bold, assertive response to Sennacherib:

> By your messengers you have ridiculed the Lord....But I know where you are and when you come and go and how you rage against me. Because you rage against me and

because your insolence has reached my ears, I will put my hook in your nose and my bit in your mouth, and I will make you return by the way you came.

—2 KINGS 19:23, 27–28, NIV

Then Isaiah released God's decree:

This is what the LORD says concerning the king of Assyria: He *will not* enter this city or shoot an arrow here. He *will not* come before it with shield or build a siege ramp against it. By the way that he came he will returnl; he will not enter this city, declares the LORD. I will defend this city and save it.

—2 KINGS 19: 32–34, NIV, EMPHASIS ADDED

As soon as Isaiah declared God's word, the armies of heaven responded to bring it to pass. "The angel of the LORD went out and put to death a hundred and eighty-five thousand in the Assyrian camp" (v. 35, NIV). After this, Sennacherib withdrew to his own land in disgrace, and when he went into the temple of his god, he was killed by two of his sons. (See 2 Kings 19:36–37.)

This is the breaker anointing in action: A decree is released from the throne of heaven, agreed with on earth, sent back to the throne of heaven, and God Himself responds. But what is a decree? It is a judicial decision or determination, a law made by a council for regulating activity within their jurisdiction. A decree is "an order, edict, or law made by a superior as a rule to govern" his subjects.[1] Robert Heidler defines a decree as "an order, edict, or rule made by one in authority resolving an issue and demanding compliance."[2]

In Luke 2:1 we find Caesar Augustus issuing a decree demanding all people to be registered. The authority of the issuer determines the power behind any decree. Because Caesar Augustus was emperor, his decree carried powerful weight. Similarly, on November 5, 2024, when the Lord told me about extending time, I knew He was preparing us for a season when heaven's decrees based on His authority would alter the destinies of America and the world.

GRACE TO TAKE THE HIGH PLACES

We are halfway through the era that began at the change of the Hebrew year in September 2019. Although we have seen much conflict, we still have a future. But what can we expect? I believe the next five-year spiritual battle for God's covenant with America will be intense. We must commit to pursuing heaven's throne, seeking to rule in alignment with God's covenant and timeline. God will give us the grace we need to do this.

I urge you to anchor your faith in the prophetic picture from Hezekiah's day. Call forth a three-year cycle of restoration so that farmland, resources, and national stability may return. Declare that by the end of this cycle, the nation will regain its right order. Invite the angel of the Lord to strike the enemy's strongholds. Assert victory and drive out unbelief, manipulation, and corruption. Use your voice and spiritual authority to set the nation's future into motion. Impart grace to others, ensuring that each believer remains standing. Strengthen one another to maintain these decrees, keeping hearts resolute and aligned with God's unfolding purposes.

The year 2025 carries two key meanings: In the Word of God, the number five is linked with grace. However, from a Hebrew understanding, it also signifies the "high places," which is why I shared in chapter 8 that we have entered a season of overthrowing our Goliaths.[3] A high place is a place of sacrifice, where blood is shed. It is where so-called ministers of the gods sacrifice to idols and create iniquitous alignments with evil.

Historically and biblically, many politically motivated kings did not fully embrace reform. Instead, they tolerated the high places, where a form of religion and worship resisted change. High places could be found on the backsides of mountains or at places where the waves of the sea met the land. There, water spirits and iniquitous, ruling land spirits aligned themselves. The collaboration of water and land spirits continues. But as we press toward our expected end, we can trust God's grace to keep us and guide us in dismantling the high places that persist in our culture and world system.

Jeremiah, who is widely believed to have written the Book of Lamentations, understood the pressures of political and spiritual conflict. Yet he continued to trust in the constancy of God's grace:

> In my mind, I keep returning to something, something that gives me hope—that the grace of ADONAI is not exhausted, that his compassion has not ended. [On the contrary,] they are new every morning! How great your faithfulness! "ADONAI I is all I have," I say; "therefore I will put my hope in him. ADONAI is good to those waiting for him, to those who are seeking him out. It is good to wait patiently for the saving help of ADONAI."
>
> —LAMENTATIONS 3:21–26, CJB

Shout "Grace!"

The unchanging God of grace supplies all you need to endure and overcome. He "is able to make all grace [every favor and earthly blessing] come in abundance to you, so that you may always [under all circumstances, regardless of the need] have complete sufficiency in everything [being completely self-sufficient in Him], and have an abundance for every good work and act of charity" (2 Cor. 9:8, AMP).

GRACE RESTORES OUR BROKEN FELLOWSHIP WITH GOD.

So, in the midst of your warring, shout "Grace!" Grace is a key attribute of God, who is "merciful and gracious, longsuffering, and abounding in goodness and truth" (Exod. 34:6). Grace is our source of help and deliverance from distress. Grace redeemed the Hebrew people from Egypt and established them in the Promised Land, in spite of their unrighteousness. (See Deuteronomy 9:5–6.) Grace sustained the early church through fierce and unrelenting persecution.

However, grace is enjoyed only within the covenant: God gifts us with grace, and we receive it through repentance and faith. (See Amos 5:14–15.) We are to seek grace humbly, praying in faith, as Malachi 1:9 reveals. God granted us the supreme revelation of His grace in the person and work of Jesus Christ, who embodied the Word of God. (See John 1:14.) To receive salvation, we must embrace Christ. (See Acts 15:11; Titus 2:11.) Grace restores our broken fellowship with God.

Whether we come to God as Jews or Gentiles, grace is applied through the Holy Spirit, who is called "the Spirit of grace" (Heb. 10:29). Grace binds us to Christ, and through Him, we receive forgiveness, adoption to sonship, newness of life, and every spiritual gift. (See Ephesians 4:7–8.)

Receive favor

The handshake of grace and favor is necessary for us to triumph. Grace is favor or kindness shown without regard to the worth or merit of the one receiving it. However, we receive favor through our acts of obedience. Favor comes when someone turns their gaze on you, and you begin to shine. Favor positions you for influence. Yet favor must be received, and that can begin only with God's grace.

I contend that you *receive* grace (2 Cor. 9:6–8; Eph. 2:8–9), *wear* favor (Ps. 5:12), and *maintain* favor by reciprocating with honor (Acts 2:46–47). I believe that if you are wearing favor, you have greater authority to release decrees. As we enter the next five years, I am trusting the Lord for the favor that each of us can wear. With the greater authority that favor brings, we can operate in kingdom force within the earth.

BEYOND OUR CONTROL

Events are happening around the world that are far beyond any person's control. Linda Heidler, one of our wonderful pastors and Robert Heidler's wife, shared the following with me:

There are two scriptures that come to my mind when I think about losing control. The first is in Psalm 2 where it says that the nations conspire together to rebel against God. For a while, God laughs at their futile plans, but then in verses 5–6 (NASB), it says, "He will speak to them in His anger and terrify them in His fury, saying, '… I have installed My King upon Zion." To me this means that a time is coming when God will begin to intervene in ways beyond the control of man, remove those who are opposing Him, and install those He chooses. The second scripture is in Isaiah 61:2 (NASB): "To proclaim the favorable year of the LORD and the day of vengeance of our God." I saw that we are in a time when this is happening with the unseating of some leaders and the reseating of others. God directly intervenes to favor some and execute vengeance on others.

Yesterday, I was reading an Israeli newsletter that had a picture of Israeli troops on Mount Hermon. The mountain was covered in snow. I immediately thought of Psalm 68:14 (NASB), "When the Almighty scattered the kings there, it was snowing in Zalmon." The psalm begins, "Let God arise, let His enemies be scattered." The whole psalm is a picture of the favor and the vengeance of God and of Him installing the king of His choosing. I saw that this process of God intervening to remove those who are opposed to Him began in June 2024, when you prophesied that God was reseating those in authority. Since that time, we have seen leader after leader removed. I'm not sure what the end result will be, but it is clear that this is God's doing.[4]

WE HAVE ENTERED A TIME OF DECREEING AND UNSEALING

After the Lord spoke to me on November 5, 2024, and told me that He was extending time, Donald Trump was elected for a second time, becoming the forty-seventh US president. Considering his first term and what God said earlier about digging around America for three and a half years, I conclude that God has extended America's timeframe to bear new fruit. President Trump started his new term of leadership by issuing executive orders to address other seasons, bring great change, unlock what had been covered over by the enemy in other times, and start a worldwide shaking of change.

Alemu Beeftu and I wrote a book called *The King's Signet Ring*, which I believe is key to understanding the major unsealing that is occurring worldwide.[5] Throughout history, kings and leaders have sealed and unsealed decrees that would set the course for the future. Ancient documents were often sealed with wax to protect and authenticate their contents and authority. The seals represented ownership; the ability to open seals signified the right to set the course and future authority of a land. The Books of Esther, Daniel, and Revelation describe sealing up revelation for a future time of unsealing—and I believe we have entered that future time!

The Book of Daniel

The Book of Daniel was written in both Hebrew and Aramaic and can be interpreted in many ways. However, the early church used this book to understand God's plan for future days. Three topics dominate its pages: the identification of kingdom wars and coming seasons of spiritual warfare, an understanding of times yet to come, and a revelation of the Ancient of Days. A realistic view of the Book of Daniel suggests it was intended to help each generation understand its own era and anticipate what would unfold in centuries ahead.

An astounding event occurs in Daniel chapters 8 and 9: Daniel experiences a visitation that leads him into intercession. In Daniel 8:16-17 the angel Gabriel appears, and in verse 18, the encounter becomes so intense that Daniel loses his strength and falls into a deep sleep. He then received an impartation of revelation and understanding that uncovered the future of nations.

Daniel not only unlocked the prophecy Jeremiah had given seventy years earlier but also sealed up revelation meant for us today. In Daniel 9:3-19 Daniel confesses the sin that led to seventy years of captivity. Then, in verses 24-27, Gabriel prophesies God's will for the future and reveals that opposition from the world would compel God's people to develop new strength and spiritual authority.

In Daniel 10:13 the Lord reveals both the Prince of Persia's resistance to Gabriel's arrival and the assistance that Gabriel receives from his fellow captain, Michael, in overcoming this opposition. Through this the Lord discloses (1) that spiritual princes would attempt to hold nations captive and block God's plan in the earth realm, and (2) that kingdom captains such as Michael and Gabriel would stand ready to help God's people.

I believe the revelation Daniel received—a revelation that was once sealed—is now being unlocked among the nations. Multitudes are in the valley of decision. We will discuss more about this season and America's role among the nations in this book's final pages.

The Book of Esther

In the Book of Esther, we see King Ahasuerus, ruler of the Persian Empire, turned against God's covenant people by his adviser Haman—a descendant of the Amalekites and a scriptural representation of the antichrist spirit. The Amalekites were Israel's staunch enemy, and like his ancestors, Haman sought to destroy God's people.

At the same time, we see God preparing and favoring a young Hebrew woman, Esther, whom He raised up to reveal the truth and expose Haman's plan to annihilate all Jews living in Persian territory. She influenced her husband, Ahasuerus, to (1) rethink decrees that he had signed at Haman's request and (2) extend favor to God's people. As a result of Esther's efforts, the king removed Haman from his position of authority and hanged him on the gallows that Haman had prepared for Esther's guardian, the godly Mordecai.

I BELIEVE THE REVELATION DANIEL RECEIVED IS NOW BEING UNLOCKED AMONG THE NATIONS.

Although the king could not cancel the decree Haman had distributed throughout the land, he issued another one granting Jews the right to war against the heads of Persian regions (Haman's ten sons) who were ready to destroy them. The Jews fought valiantly, and God's kingdom was extended! I believe this shows that, at times, God's people must be willing to go to war and undo wrongful operations against God's plan on the earth.

Since Donald Trump has become our forty-seventh president, I believe that he will encourage kingdoms to go to war—sometimes by encouraging battles and at other times by bringing preexisting spiritual battles to light. Through his executive orders, many decrees and documents that have been wrongly sealed and are operating against the plan of God will come to light and be overturned and reversed.

The sealing of evil decrees is not new. In 1 Kings 21:8 Jezebel made decrees and sealed them on Ahab's behalf. These decrees were empowered by a ruling supernatural force called Baal, which sought to stop the advance of God's remnant people. This perhaps parallels the past seventy years in America, in which many wicked decrees have gone forth. However, we have entered the season for overthrowing them.

The Book of Revelation

The Revelation of Jesus Christ, which centers on John's imprisonment on Patmos and visitation from the Lord, is also a key book for us to understand currently. In Revelation, John is more closely aligned with Isaiah than with Daniel, and he leads us through many scenarios of what will be unsealed in the days ahead. Warfare will become intense: The light will become lighter, and the darkness will become darker.

John begins the book by evaluating the seven key churches in Asia Minor. I believe God will examine each territory in our world over the next three and a half years, beginning from the writing of this book. He will determine in which places and ways His people are exercising His authority. My favorite chapter of Revelation—chapter 12—points to the coming of a new move and birth that will result in great warfare. However, God's people will triumph due to their testimony, Christ's blood, and the casting off of their worldly cares, which enables them to seek His kingdom first.

These three books—Daniel, Esther, and Revelation—speak to aspects of our times and to the matter of sealing and unsealing documents and decrees. However, my understanding of this matter is also linked to Jesus' crucifixion and burial in a sealed and guarded tomb. Although the authorities exercised every measure to seal His testimony of the future, God unsealed the tomb. Our Messiah rose and imparted an anointing to those who had walked with Him for three years. He then left the person of His Spirit to empower a remnant to bring heaven into the earth realm from generation to generation. Today, the remnant of God is now arising to demonstrate His power amid the earthly war.

WHAT ABOUT ISRAEL? WHAT ABOUT AMERICA?

When reading Esther, Daniel, and Revelation, I sensed the Lord opening my eyes to how He is sorting out the nations. America, Russia, China, Iraq, Iran, Taiwan, Ukraine, Cuba, and many other nations are being assessed to see whether they will allow God's remnant to arise or will try to stop any move of His Spirit in the earth.

All nations will eventually gather around God's covenant nation, Israel. Israel is a hammer in the Middle East—a kind of David amid the Goliaths, striking at strongholds no one else will face. When Israel entered the Promised Land, each tribe was called to war for their inheritance. Some, like Caleb, did so; others did not. Caleb asked for the upper and lower springs of his portion of land. "Therefore, Hebron became {his} inheritance...because he followed the LORD, the God of Israel, completely. The name of Hebron was formerly Kiriath-arba [city of Arba]; for Arba was the greatest man among the [giant-like] Anakim. Then the land had rest from war" (Josh. 14:14–15, AMP).

Earlier in the Book of Joshua, we see a different result regarding giants: "There were no Anakim left in the land of the children of Israel; *only in Gaza, in Gath, and in Ashdod* [of Philistia] *some remained*" (Josh. 11:22, AMP, emphasis added). Judah was allotted much land to fully occupy, including Jerusalem. However, Joshua 15:63 (AMP) says that "the [tribe of the] sons of Judah were not able to drive them {the Jebusites} out; so the Jebusites live with the sons of Judah in Jerusalem to this day."

My point is that unless strongholds are confronted, they maintain their hold. In the current season, many strongholds have yet to be challenged and must be addressed. Therefore, we see unrest and war and a world focused on Gaza and Jerusalem as focal points of coming global conflict. A superhighway of war is already taking shape: Russia, Iran, and Syria are joining forces to create a pathway for world war. Daniel prophesied this, and John witnessed it when he was caught up into the heavens. Many nations are choosing which path they will follow—the path of the goat nations or the sheep nations.

So where does America stand? Remember what God showed me: He has extended America's influence for what lies ahead. I believe that continued influence requires America to remain in relationship with Israel. As I read the Book of Daniel, I saw America and Russia in conflict over Israel in the future.

I believe that America's transition and increased influence will bring division. The question is whether America will embrace or withdraw from what God is orchestrating. Any true shift will ask something of both the nation and the church, because change and uncertainty are not always welcomed. Considering these dynamics, let's better grasp what it means to shift by looking at the *Merriam-Webster* definitions of the verb *shift*:

- "To change the place, position, or direction of" something

- "To exchange for or replace by another"

- "To change gears" (to accelerate, for example)[6]

A *shift* can mean changing place, position, or direction; exchanging one way for another; or adjusting speed and momentum. It can also refer to a designated period of work or "a deceitful or underhand scheme."[7] Remember, the enemy is actively plotting to stop the shift that God desires and substitute it with his evil schemes.

When a true shift occurs, it often brings secondary effects, such as a shaking. Think of a geological fault line: The ground shifts and divides, forming a rift. Spiritually, God has appointed seasons when division is necessary for His covenant to emerge in a new way. Such shifts may produce rifts in relationships, society, and many areas of life. Jesus said, "I came not to send peace, but a sword" (Matt. 10:34, KJV). Let's make sure that, as members of God's kingdom, we do not use the sword against one another!

A time comes when you emerge from a transition—when you can no longer keep prophesying that the new will happen, because *it is already unfolding*. At that point you must face the difficulties of change and allow everything within you to embrace it.

This is what we in America are called to do. It is time to fully embrace the shift we are in.

WATERS OF CHANGE: A SHIFTING, RIFT-CUTTING RIVER

A time also comes when the waters of change begin to rise and produce a river. Rivers are powerful—they flow! Sometimes they flow like torrents; other times they are less forceful and choppier.

MANY NATIONS ARE CHOOSING WHICH PATH THEY WILL FOLLOW—THE PATH OF THE GOAT NATIONS OR THE SHEEP NATIONS.

Several years ago I met Pam and some of our children at the Grand Canyon, a natural wonder of the world. While standing at an incredible viewpoint on the rim, I heard the Spirit of God say, "A new type of river is now rising in this land. This river will create a schism unlike anything this nation has ever known before."

I realized we must get ready, because our nation will no longer be as we have known it. The Lord added, "I have brought you into a season of the new wineskin. Tell My people to be prepared for structures to change. This nation [America] is a wineskin, and it will change."

As I stood on the canyon's rim, viewing the magnificence of God's power and creation, I saw a vision of a nation divided. God has dealt with me, as an intercessor, to be prepared for a great schism in America. What we see unfold in the natural will soon become spiritual as well.

The Grand Canyon itself seemed to illustrate this coming schism. The canyon was likely formed when the Colorado River began to flow—and *wow*—the river cut through rock, changing the land forever. The waters opened a rift, resembling nothing that came before and nothing that may come again.

I heard the Lord say, "That is the type of river that is coming. It will seem devastating to some and refreshing to others, but it will bring you to a new place of harvest. How you process the changes will determine how well you are prepared for the future. You can choose to be on either side of the rift, or you can get in the river and travel to your next destination amid the land's changing course!"

The key in this season is to remember that the river *will* create rifts. The river of God is stirring the "fish" within it and carving a new pathway for their future habitation. Therefore, the church must adapt its structure while preparing for the river to run its course and bring a new supply of fish into our nets. So let's mend our nets, recognizing the changing times and season. If we wade into the rising river creatively and not in fear, the Lord will fill our nets!

YOU CHOOSE: SCHISM OR RIFT

America is marked by schisms. Washington, DC, is a political war zone. So how will the schism be bridged? Will the election of one president accomplish this? I believe the answer is no. We must move beyond political discourse and release our idealized notions of freedom. Instead of focusing on schisms, we must confront a harsh reality: a rift in our nation.

A *schism* is "a division or disunion, esp. into mutually opposed parties."[8] In ecclesiastical terms a schism occurs when a formal separation happens over a doctrinal or administrative difference between sects or denominations. This triggers offense and division, and division is the opposite of multiplication.

In his first letter to the Corinthians, Paul warned against schisms within the church:

> Now indeed there are many members, yet one body. And the eye cannot say to the hand, "I have no need of you"; nor again the head to the feet, "I have no need of you." No, much rather, those members of the body which seem to be weaker are necessary. And those members of the body which we

think to be less honorable, on these we bestow greater honor; and our unpresentable parts have greater modesty, but our presentable parts have no need. But God composed the body, having given greater honor to that part which lacks it, that there should be no schism in the body, but that the members should have the same care for one another. And if one member suffers, all the members suffer with it; or if one member is honored, all the members rejoice with it.

—1 CORINTHIANS 12:20–26

Rifts can go beyond the division caused by schisms. *To rift* means "to burst open" or "divide."[9] A rift is an opening made by splitting—like the formation of the Grand Canyon—or it can occur from a break in friendly relations or a difference of opinion. It's possible to agree to disagree without condemning one another.

In a world filled with schisms, I see a rift—a bursting open of our future as the river of God flows from the heavenly realm, carving out a new place for us to stand. From this new ground, we can call out for His power and glory to come into the earth.

In Scripture, rivers and waters frequently symbolize the following benefits:

- Abundance—especially the abundance of God's grace (Ps. 36:8; 46:4; Isa. 32:2; 41:18; John 7:38)

- Peace (Isa. 66:12)

- The blessings or good things of life (Job 20:17; 29:6)

- God's providence and provision (Isa. 43:19–20)

- The fruitfulness of trees planted by rivers, representing the lasting prosperity of the righteous (Ps. 1:3; Jer. 17:8)

Rivers and waters can also symbolize negative outcomes:

- Affliction or distress (Ps. 69:2; Isa. 43:2)

- God's judgment—such as the drying up of rivers (Isa. 19:1–8; Jer. 51:36; Nah. 1:4; Zech. 10:11) or their overflowing beyond their intended boundaries (Isa. 8:7–8; 28:2, 17; Jer. 47:2)

How the water gushes or flows can reveal a message from the Creator to His people. These waters bursting forth from the rift provide a window for harvest, and it is critical that we understand how to enter the harvest waters at this moment in history. This is a time for violent praise. We must learn to praise our way through every obstacle. Merely declaring the name of God causes a violent reaction from the enemy. When we praise, we wield a mighty weapon in the heavenly places. We are living in violent times, so praise violently! Your violent praise is preparing a storehouse for kingdom harvest. The river of God must rise—otherwise, we will not see the bursting open of His plans for this nation.

IF WE WADE INTO THE RISING RIVER CREATIVELY AND NOT IN FEAR, THE LORD WILL FILL OUR NETS!

The US is a nation of many factions. But God's river is life, and His life always overcomes death. America needs a fresh release of His kingdom river. Ezekiel 47:9 says, "Every living thing that moves, wherever the rivers go, will live." This river has the power to heal nations. (See Ezekiel 47:12; Revelation 22:1–2.)

Saying we need a release of the river of God is another way of saying we need a fresh outpouring of His Spirit. Nothing else will break the spirit of death and political schism that is rising in this land. We must return to the Lord and repent—that is, choose a new way of thinking. We must repent for divisive political leanings that prevent us from representing the God of righteousness in our choices. As a nation among nations, we must always represent His kingdom in our actions here on earth.

What do we believe, and what will shape our thinking as we raise future generations? We are contending with the concept of enlightenment, which elevates human reason above divine revelation. Meanwhile, America's founding concept of democracy is eroding. However, God intended for the ecclesia (the church) to have the greatest influence. The church in America must become an apostolic force producing change in our nation, because true enlightenment comes from the Light of the world.

Our Constitution and Declaration of Independence establish the United States as a republic with a voice. How we use that voice is what matters most. To use it well, we must **AMERICA IS TORN BY ANTICHRIST IDEOLOGY.** acknowledge our current state. This means stepping back and recognizing we have never been this way before. As with Joshua after Moses's passing, America's current leaders must seek wisdom each day about the changes required.

America is torn by antichrist ideology. Yet I see a remnant rising and growing strong. The voice of this remnant must continue to be heard in the days ahead. For America to triumph and for God's glory to be extended to the next three generations, the Trump administration must continue to favor the voice of the kingdom.

HOW COULD UKRAINE CREATE A RIFT IN AMERICA?

One of the major divisions in America today involves the nation of Ukraine. The US established diplomatic relations with Ukraine in 1991, following Ukraine's independence from the Soviet Union.[10] The US places great importance on the success of Ukraine's transition to a modern democratic state with a flourishing market economy.

I have been to Ukraine several times. In 2008 Dr. Peter Wagner convened a meeting of apostles from across the nations of the former Soviet Union. Thirty-six leaders from seven nations gathered for a peer-level meeting to share and receive revelation for the future. The former Soviet Bloc countries had long been controlled by oppressive mindsets and philosophies, and until 1990, nationalism was the primary "religion." Of course, the Russian Orthodox Church and Roman Catholicism were the major religious structures, and they remain predominate forces.

But God! The Lord is raising a new level of apostolic leadership in these nations. Leaders from Russia, Belarus, Latvia, and Poland, as well as other cities and nations, attended the meeting. At the outset of our introductions, each one acknowledged that the mindset of the former Soviet Union still existed in these lands. By the afternoon of the first day, the Spirit of God began to move greatly.

In 1983 the Lord called me to pray for former Soviet nations, although a major event—the fall of the Berlin Wall—would not occur until November 1989. In 1990 the Lord showed me that a wave of oppression had been stilled to give these nations a window of awakening. But He also revealed that another wave of oppression would come. Ezra 9:8 (NIV) says, "But now, for a brief moment, the LORD our God has been gracious in leaving us a remnant and giving us a firm place in his sanctuary, and so our God gives light to our eyes and a little relief in our bondage."

An apostolic-prophetic base must be established so that the people in former Soviet Bloc lands can withstand the next wave of bondage. The approaching oppression will be more dangerous and rigid than the previous one, which restricted the church for seventy years. A lack of apostolic-prophetic structure in these nations has existed until now, so establishing one is necessary to fully break them free of the legalistic religious structure of the past. Our meeting in 2008 represented a new breed of leaders and brought much encouragement for the harvest ahead in these lands. However, these nations must seize the window of opportunity now opening for the church's establishment.

During the 2008 meeting, the Lord began to speak:

> The same spirit that operated in the days of Esther, the Haman spirit, has resided in the former Soviet Bloc nations. But I am raising up a group of leaders who will receive strategy to overthrow this Haman force. Begin now to join hands and move with Me in ways you have never moved before. A new wave of oppression is coming upon your horizon that will overcome you unless you dig deep now. Your confrontation must go deep. Prepare for a great harvest! For this wave of governmental

control will have a supernatural dimension, empowering civil government with occult forces that will attempt to annihilate My church. My kingdom is a kingdom that cannot be stopped. However, this is a time when you must have revelation power to truly demonstrate My authority. This will be as in the days of Moses. If you will embrace My fire in a new way, you will overthrow the structure forming against you. I say signs and wonders will come to these lands and begin to break the powers that are arising. This will be a season of apostolic confrontation for My church and its leaders.

We observed the movement of the Spirit among the Jewish people within Ukraine, which would infuriate the civil government. The church would rise to support the Messianic church. In Russia a new expression of the "one new man" will emerge (Eph. 2:15). A window is forming in the heavens over the former Soviet Bloc nations.

RUSSIA IS A STRONGHOLD OF CONTENTION

Russia remains a Goliath on the world stage. We must use declaration and proclamation to exercise our governmental authority. The church must continue to arise and acknowledge the real wars we are facing from the world's governments.

For example, Ezekiel 37–38 reveals Russia's conflicting stance against God's covenant nation of Israel. God told Ezekiel, "Son of man, set your face against Gog of the land of Magog, the chief ruler of Meshech and Tubal, and prophesy against him, and say, 'Thus says the Lord God, "Behold, I am against you, O Gog, chief ruler of Meshech and Tubal"'" (vv. 38:2–3, AMP). In the days ahead, a conspiracy will be uncovered in Gog and Magog. This will manifest in two ways: (1) through trade transactions between the Black Sea and the Persian Gulf and (2) through an anti-Semitic political conspiracy targeting God's covenant plan.

Let me list the structures that stop spiritual breakthrough in this region of the world. As is true of the Prince of Persia, each of these areas in Russia have princes ruling with the following influences:

- spirit of Cain

- spirit of Sophia (wisdom and religion)

- spirit of fear and intimidation

- demons of deception: They are linked to erroneous doctrines the church has embraced, which have lulled us into patiently waiting for Jesus' return rather than taking up our governmental authority to war for societal transformation. This deception can be defeated through education and training.

The spirit of Cain

To tear down a stronghold, you must first define it. Let's explore the spirit of Cain, which I believe is the root from which communism, other philosophies, and ruling powers have sprung. Reviewing Cain's life and characteristics will help us fathom the workings of this spirit:

- Cain was the firstborn, but he forfeited his firstborn rights. (See Genesis 4:1–12.)

- Cain lost the firstfruits anointing and did not gain God's favor when he withheld his best offering, allowing anger to rule his heart. (See Genesis 4:3–5.)

- Cain was the first murderer. (See Genesis 4:8.)

- Cain was the first to be sent out from God's presence, as recorded in Genesis 4:16. (Adam and Eve tried to hide from God's presence in Genesis 3:8, but that was their choice. In Genesis 3:23–24, God sent them out from the garden but not from His presence.)

- Cain was the first person to have a curse pronounced on him. (See Genesis 4:11.)

- Cain was the first to have his conscience seared for shedding Abel's blood. The sound of Abel's blood crying out from the ground tormented Cain.

- Cain was a wandering exile—a fugitive unable to establish roots.

- Cain was an exile in the land of Nod, which may have been in the Persian Gulf region. (See Genesis 4:16.) From there I believe Cain's descendants moved to Magog and Gog, likely north of Nod—connecting the spirit of Cain to these lands.

To overthrow the spirit of Cain requires

- reversing the curse that has blocked the double portion in these lands;

- remaining vigilant for political conspiracies unique to these regions;

- recognizing, as God's covenant people, that ongoing war with political structures will continue;

- rising as God's apostolic people—with strength to proclaim truth and stand firm against political conspiracies;

- for those in the affected regions: not growing weary amid political struggles, trusting the Lord's protection, and presenting His covenant throughout the region.

The real war for the church in this region is fought to bring God's presence where Cain's spirit prevails. Cain was religious but acted outside God's presence, creating an order contrary to God's intention. This was unprecedented. Thus, the Cain principle is a firstfruits principle. In God's kingdom order, apostles are first in order and serve as prototypes (1 Cor. 12:28). The Cain spirit will be overthrown only when apostolic anointing rises to a new dimension in these lands. Not only must apostles rise, but the church must become an apostolic church—able to withstand ongoing political turmoil.

THE FUTURE

There is a key connection between the Black Sea and the Persian Gulf. Therefore, Ukraine can impact the apostolic in Persian Gulf nations. Ukraine also has the potential to effect change in Syria. We decree that all false worship systems be overthrown so the presence of God can be fully restored in the church throughout these regions. The church must rise and uproot the communistic mentality from this region so that many may be delivered.

THE REAL WAR FOR THE CHURCH IS FOUGHT TO BRING GOD'S PRESENCE WHERE CAIN'S SPIRIT PREVAILS.

I believe this deliverance will open the window for harvest. This will prompt a political confrontation between the governments and the church in the region—a confrontation that will be heard worldwide. These opposing powers are headed for the greatest clash ever. What makes this different from confrontations of the 1960s, 1970s, and 1980s is the current apostolic order and authority. In the past the church often succumbed to changes; but in this new era, the region's church will gain ground—and I believe its voice will be heard.

Clearly, we must war for the apostolic church to rise with great strength in regions dominated by the Cain spirit. When this rising occurs, this generation's church will carry such a presence of God that it will become unafraid to confront political structures. Do not be deceived by political systems in regions where the spirit of Cain is entrenched. Because of that spirit, the roots of murder and anti-Semitism continue to deepen in the land, and the structure will always conspire against God's covenant plan—including the church and the Abrahamic covenant linked to the Jewish people.

When the apostolic authority of the region's church rises to a new level, it will no longer be divided. Instead, a corporate anointing will release demonstrative power. The region will be "as in the days of Moses," with great demonstrations from heaven to earth. Even now, God is raising many new leaders whom He has prepared for this kind of demonstration.

THE TIME HAS COME FOR THE CHURCH TO RISE AND PUT ON A NEW APOSTOLIC MANTLE THROUGHOUT THE ENTIRE BLOC OF FORMER SOVIET NATIONS.

I urge you to pray prophetically over Ezekiel 38. The time has come for the church to rise and put on a new apostolic mantle throughout the entire bloc of former Soviet nations. Give thanks that the church will advance and not retreat. Ask the Lord to raise and establish a thousand apostolic leaders across the region and to anoint them with power for demonstration. Call forth Nebuchadnezzars and Dariuses throughout the political structures. Declare that the Lord will favor the church in the region so it can gain new footing.

Declare that the church will be victorious against the alliance of secular and political spirits. Proclaim that the government of God will penetrate the political system, arts, social system, spiritual system, and every area of life and dominion. Declare that the spirit of communism will be rendered powerless and ineffective against the church. Pray for the church in that region, as it must war to break down the spirit of anti-Semitism. A new form of worship must sweep the region. Historically, Abraham received revelation of the Lord from the line of Abel, not Cain. The war over worship in that whole region must turn now.

A TIME TO USE PROPHETIC REVELATION

Yes, let us know (recognize, be acquainted with, and understand) Him; let us be zealous to know the Lord [to appreciate, give heed to, and cherish Him]. His going forth is prepared and certain as the dawn, and He will come to us as the [heavy] rain, as the latter rain that waters the earth.
—Hosea 6:3, AMPC

We have much intercession at Global Spheres Center, where Lisa Lyons recently had this revelation:

People often rant and rave about the evils of "one-world government," yet God fashioned the earth for just such a system. It was His intent from the beginning. All of creation in the earth and beyond is hardwired to be ordered by and respond to one ruling structure. I don't think we realize how literal this is. Within every created thing, there are forces pressing for the manifestation of one-world government, much like in the series *The Lord of the Rings*, with the One Ring seeking to return to its master, Sauron. It is the mold into which all creation was made to fit. It is part of the cry Paul speaks of in Romans 8:22. It is the fullness of intent and identity for the earth and everything in it.

Our opportunistic enemy has been very adept at exploiting and capitalizing on the principles God put in place for one-world government, seeking to make himself the "one" at the top. But those same principles are available for us to utilize in establishing "on earth as it is in heaven." Creation is waiting to help us bring into manifestation the reign of Lord Yeshua in one ruling structure over all the earth....I also believe that in all the enemy's schemes and manipulations, he is only setting the stage for Yeshua's triumph. He may structure a government and fashion a throne, but he will never sit on it.... He'll simply get it all in place for Yeshua to step in and take over. He is playing into God's purposes just like at the cross."[11]

It is time to apply prophetic revelation. Think of Daniel in exile in Babylon. He thrived among, and excelled in, the powerful pagan society of Babylonia. Daniel worshipped the God of his forefathers and surpassed the understanding of Babylonian magicians, as much as Moses outwitted Pharaoh's sorcerers.

In Daniel 2:18, after Nebuchadnezzar's magicians, astrologers, and sorcerers failed to interpret the king's dream, Daniel asked the king for time to interpret the dream, and he and his companions began to "seek mercies from the God of heaven concerning this [dream]." They knew that unless God answered their prayers, they, too, would be executed. "Then the secret was revealed to Daniel in a night vision. So Daniel blessed the God of heaven" (v. 19).

DON'T LET FEAR KEEP YOU FROM YOUR ASSIGNMENT.

As we move forward, we must learn from Daniel. As we wait, watch, and follow the Lord's leading about how and when to act, let's remember these vital lessons from Daniel chapter 2:

- Take time to hear clearly from the Lord, just as Daniel did when he asked Nebuchadnezzar for time to seek God (v. 16).

- Find like-minded believers who will press into God and pray with you in this new season (vv. 17–18).

- Have faith that God will meet you in your sphere of assignment and authority, and trust that the secret will be revealed as the Lord chooses. This might happen through prayer, the Word, other believers, or—like Daniel—through a prophetic dream or other revelation (v. 19).

- And most importantly, bless the God of heaven for new revelation, for a new season, and for His goodness (v. 19).

In the cultural and spiritual Babylon in which we live, we must be like Daniel. He gained such favor with the pagan king that he was able to save the magicians' lives. (See Daniel 2:24–25.) He didn't use the magicians' type of access to revelation; he transcended it in the spirit realm and returned to apply it in the earth realm. That is exactly what we need to do.

God has shown us things beyond 2026! Don't let fear keep you from your assignment. Are you afraid because you anticipate lack in the future? Do you worry about being ill-equipped for the war ahead? You need not worry or concern yourself about tomorrow. Simply act on your path! Keep moving with God, and He will show you everything you need.

CHAPTER 10

2026 AND BEYOND: WHAT WILL BECOME OF US?

I N THIS FINAL chapter, I wish to encourage you to see ahead. Don't stop now—keep advancing! This book cannot cover every detail of the challenges ahead. Perhaps I will share more as events proceed. Listening daily to what the Spirit of the Lord is saying to the church is my practice. Just remember this: There will always be "wars and rumors of wars" (Matt. 24:6). Therefore, don't become anxious over every skirmish, retaliation, and threat.

However, there are three battlefields to watch closely: Russia and Ukraine, China and Taiwan, and, of course, Israel and the Middle East. Israel is the most important focus, and America still holds the greatest influence, but the danger I saw in 1986 was that America would lose her influence.

The greatest need I sense for every saint on earth is to keep their hearts pure, so they "will see God" (Matt. 5:8, NIV). In seeing Him, our discernment will remain sharp, our strength will hold, our love will burn passionately, and our confidence will endure.

ALLOWING THE LORD TO EXTEND US INTO THE FUTURE WITHOUT FEAR

I think the most common fear that people express is rooted in their confusion about the future. "What if?" they ask. "Could this happen?" they wonder. Some people see so many things manifesting in the world that they consider staying indoors and shielding themselves from chaos. They worry about provision in the days ahead, fear making a mistake and not being able to recover, and wonder if they will miss the path to their destiny. They ask, "Do I really have a future?"

These are valid questions and concerns. However, we must remember what the Lord said, "Do not worry about tomorrow; for tomorrow will worry about itself. Each day has enough trouble of its own" (Matt. 6:34, AMP). The dilemma we face is learning to see our future without letting fear cloud our vision or deter us from our destiny. As our time together closes, I want to assure you that you *can* see your future without fear.

THE DILEMMA WE FACE IS LEARNING TO SEE OUR FUTURE WITHOUT LETTING FEAR CLOUD OUR VISION OR DETER US FROM OUR DESTINY.

When we look into the future, we do it with *foresight* or *foreknowledge*. To understand these nouns, we must recognize both the predictive and analytical quality of each. We humans gather information and acquire knowledge, but both must be analyzed. We are gifted with discernment and the intuitive ability to sense that something will happen. Both foresight and foreknowledge are important for embracing our best future, and thoughtful questions can uncover insights. Wisdom learned from past associations and situations helps us develop long-range perception. However, revelation uncovers the steps that cause us to finish strong and receive God's acclamation, "Well done, good and faithful servant" (Matt. 25:21).

When we reflect on our future, we need to express gratitude for everything we have already experienced. As I wrote in chapter 2, our core values help form our thought processes. Our core values and gratitude for what we have are both involved in looking forward to a place we have never reached and walking in a way we have never walked.

To embrace the future that we see by the Spirit, we must develop action steps—each driven by confidence in the future success of the mission we seek to accomplish. Therefore, we must meditate on our steps—both those from the past and those leading into the unknown. We must rehearse and remember our "wins" and our "losses," because we learn from both.

We need to practice and experiment until we are surer of the steps ahead. However, a moment comes when we must exert our will and choose; we must take a step that results in an immediate action. We cannot go through life saying, "I am about to do such and so," or "One day this will happen." Each day contains moments when we must choose. When we do, the path ahead opens, and we see further than we did the day before.

ARE YOU JUST WAITING FOR THE RAPTURE?

As previously mentioned, I did not grow up immersed in religion or the church world. But at times I attended church with my grandmother and mother, whose denomination of choice was Baptist. I did not understand their ways, but I noticed that the church was not saturated with Baptist theology or demonstration. They were proponents of the Word who welcomed certain manifestations. I still remember how they prayed for the sick and prophesied.

When Pam and I married, we continued to meet with young, married couples at the Baptist Student Union of Texas A&M in College Station. Occasionally, we visited other churches in the area, including Catholic, Lutheran, Methodist, and other Baptist churches. We even visited a Church of Christ with a married couple we knew. My point is that I gained a broad perspective of the church. We also met in our home with several Spirit-filled couples, as I had been baptized in the Holy Spirit during this season.

Pam and I did not commit to church life until 1978, at which time God led us to a large Baptist church in Houston that was moving in renewal. However, I had not previously been introduced to the aspect of their theology that involved what they called *the rapture*. Whenever the topic of the rapture arose, they discussed what would become of us all. Yet, as they presented it, this theology did not resonate within me.

By then I knew from the Word of God that Enoch went up, Elijah was caught up in a fiery chariot, Jesus ascended, and Stephen witnessed the glory of God just before he was martyred by stoning. (See Genesis 5:24; 2 Kings 2:11; Luke 24:50–51; Acts 7:55–56.) When I listened to church discussions, someone would eventually say, "We have a call in the earth realm to endure and demonstrate the power of God for those around us to see." As I read the New Testament from start to finish for perhaps the fifth time, I saw how testimony and demonstration of the good news changed entire regions. I finally concluded that we were not called simply to dwell on escaping the world; we were called to be in the world but not conformed to the world.

Approximately fifty years have passed since then, and I am even more convinced that we are not here to escape but to walk in the Spirit and demonstrate the Lord's goodness to those around us. In the midst of trials, we are to continue walking. When we are persecuted, we are to continue walking. As Isaiah 58:8 says, "Your righteousness shall go before you; the glory of the LORD shall be your rear guard." Therefore, the need to be raptured never became a driving force in my life. The need to walk with Him has become my daily motivation. I know that my spirit will eventually be present with the Lord, whether through death or being caught away in some manner. In the meantime my spirit needs to live in a rapturous zone with Him every day. Then I will transition in His perfect timing.

So how do we face the future on a day-to-day, moment-to-moment basis? How do we answer the question "What will become of me?" Since the day our Lord ascended, His church has anticipated a "catching away." Nothing is wrong with expecting a tremendous conflict between good and evil, but if you lose touch with the "day of the Lord" and the day in which you are currently living, you will find yourself deluded and hopeless. Why? Because we have not been left here to seek our exit. We have been left here to accomplish a purpose—from one generation to the next—until He comes again!

WALKING FORWARD IN THE DAYS AHEAD

Having come this far in this book, you can probably tell that the Lord has developed in me a vision of the world, of Him, and of Jesus as the King of the kingdom. I am humbled that He has granted me—and made real to me—a level of understanding regarding kingdom realities and principles.

We need to understand the difference between the kingdom and the church. The word for church is *ecclesia*, which denotes a governing body. Jesus prophesied this in Matthew 16:18–19, and we are still becoming what He prophesied. The kingdom is the whole of God's redeeming activity in Christ, expressed throughout the world. He is working though us to influence the structures of society. Once we give our lives to Him and embrace His Spirit, the kingdom dwells in us.

The church is the assembly of those who belong to Christ Jesus. Dutch Sheets said that the kingdom takes visible form in those who have assembled as the church. As we make this shift in our understanding, we will start manifesting the reality of God's kingdom. When we assemble together, we should have much greater power than what we exhibit alone. We need to ask God to shift us into a greater holy array so that He can come and meet us in a new way.

Kingdom people are sent out to do kingdom work. As kingdom representatives advance, they meet opposing forces. Kingdom people understand this warfare and do not back away from it. They know that kingdoms are embroiled in conflict, so they learn to navigate spiritual battles. They are not focused on self-preservation; rather, each time they step out the door, they do so with a sense of mission and assignment.

We have been given grace and faith to overcome the antichrist forces. Our call to change the world around us is a driving force. Since I was a young boy, I knew my call was beyond my hometown, and I feel just as comfortable worshiping in Africa or Asia as I do in Texas. However, I love attending the church at our apostolic kingdom center. I *see* the kingdom of God manifesting from nation to nation, and no matter where I am assigned or walk, I know I need to represent Him.

To that end I serve as an apostle, sending teams into diverse harvest fields. These teams engage in a wide range of activities—from sports activities and farm management to city governments. We have teams that meet with national leaders and teams that meet with educators, with whom we regularly pray. In fact, we consider the schoolteacher's mission to be among the highest callings in today's society.

The Spirit of God is currently developing apostolic centers where His kingdom can be both displayed and demonstrated. The Lord not only declares His Word but performs His Word and manifests His glory. These centers are prototypes—demonstrations of what heaven discloses for the earth! At one time we had forty teams participating in bowling associations throughout the entire Dallas Metroplex. One elder's daughter served as head cheerleader for the Dallas Cowboys, so we sent teams to pray and attend home games. We have teams of Spirit-empowered women who go to strip clubs each week to minister to the workers. We now associate with 450 children whose mothers are in this occupation.

WE CONSIDER THE SCHOOLTEACHER'S MISSION TO BE AMONG THE HIGHEST CALLINGS IN TODAY'S SOCIETY.

I really can't think of any group or mission field to which the Lord could not assign us as witnesses to His love. The overall goal is to go where He sends us, proclaim His grace, show love to others, and reveal a more excellent way of life. We are called to be in the harvest to serve as harvesters for God's kingdom!

WE ARE A FIERCE AND RISING REMNANT

So what will happen to us, and where do we go from here? The Lord has already answered these questions from a big-picture perspective, both in the Old Testament and the New:

"They will be my people," says the LORD of Heaven's Armies. "On the day when I act in judgment, they will be my own special treasure. I will spare them as a father spares an obedient child. Then you will again see the difference between the righteous and the wicked, between those who serve God and those who do not."

—MALACHI 3:17–18, NLT

But it is no shame to suffer for being a Christian. Praise God for the privilege of being called by his name! For the time has come for judgment, and it must begin with God's household. And if judgment begins with us, what terrible fate awaits those who have never obeyed God's Good News?

—1 PETER 4:16–17, NLT

As the apostle Peter wrote, "Praise God for the privilege of being called by his name!" even if we must suffer for belonging to Him. In every generation God raises a remnant—those who carry and communicate His prophetic will, ensuring that heaven's purposes continue to break into and impact the earth realm. This remnant preserves His covenant. (See Acts 9:15.)

The remnant is saved out of the unbelieving world. They remain uncompromising and distinct in their pursuit of God's will. (See Romans 9:27.) This group is growing daily, becoming an even greater force than the early church was. (See 2 Corinthians 10:15.)

I believe Jesus birthed this remnant during His travail in Gethsemane. Since then, God has set apart people in every generation for His purpose—those who remain in the land, understand His will, and stay committed to their calling. They labor to accomplish what previous generations did not complete. Among them are prophets who declare what will last and be handed down to those who come after. In every age a faithful group endures calamity and remains called by the Lord. They are the anointed ones who escape judgment to spread the good news and bear witness of "Jacob's trouble" (Jer. 30:7).

A remnant will always wage wars against the false witness, the accuser, and the antichrist. When this remnant is no more, the final war will occur.

> Let no one in any way deceive or entrap you, for that day will not come unless the apostasy comes first [that is, the great rebellion, the abandonment of the faith by professed Christians], and the man of lawlessness is revealed, the son of destruction [the Antichrist, the one who is destined to be destroyed].
>
> —2 THESSALONIANS 2:3, AMP

So chill out. We'll be here for a while.

"THE ONE THOUSAND DAYS AHEAD"

In January 2025, the Lord awakened me and said, "I will show you the one thousand days ahead, if you wish to see!" I responded with caution. The Lord desires to reveal many things to us, but true wisdom begins with acknowledging, respecting, and revering Him. We must bear in mind Jeremiah 33:3 (AMP): "Call to Me and I will answer you, and tell you [and even show you] great and mighty things, [things which have been confined and hidden], which you do not know and understand and cannot distinguish."

Here are a few developments I see ahead, starting from January 20, 2025:

- Elections in America are triggering a domino effect of dramatic changes in national leadership worldwide. God will present Himself to nations, and each nation will need to choose its alignment according to covenant with the God of Israel.

- A new identity is emerging in President Trump: He will transition from the role of Cyrus to that of Darius. Cyrus was anointed and chosen for Israel's sake. (See Isaiah 45:4.) This was the beginning of presenting salvation to nations that would not receive it. (See Isaiah 45:4–14).

The US president must choose to align himself with Israel, much like Darius did with Daniel, and must remain connected to God's kingdom people. Darius observed whether Daniel could endure the lion's den; similarly, as we face our own lion's den experiences, we have an advocate standing with us. The US president must supernaturally recognize God's favor on His people and choose to stand by them.

- Media rule must yield to God's authority. Daniel's experience in the lion's den marked the unraveling of the Persian goddess Anahita's influence, as Daniel's presence silenced accusations. Today's media and communication battles will lead to changes in news systems and more open confession of God.

- Key global trade routes should be monitored, as corruption in trading will generate a worldwide upheaval for 490 days. This event echoes when Lucifer was cast out of heaven due to "the iniquity of [his] trading" (Ezek. 28:18). Expect this trading turmoil to endure for the 490-day period.

- God's kingdom people—the "shining ones"—will rise during the harvest, shining with greater brilliance than before. Intense opposition and clear divide will emerge between evil and those who carry God's glory. This will bring a season of insult, accusation, and persecution, but God's true remnant will be revealed.

- Religion must be overcome for the supernatural power of God to arise and shape the church's future. Religion will resist the next supernatural move of God, but the remnant must dismantle controlling powers and stand firm in every circumstance. The prophetic voice must become clear, sharp, and decisive. Territorial breakthrough will come as the church confesses to quenching Holy Spirit in prior seasons. The current administration of the church must allow space for Holy Spirit to manifest in fresh, new ways. The remnant must pursue and uncover revelation still hidden in the Word, activating the spirit realm among believers.

- The Spirit of revelation for the next three and a half years is already being released. Open your mouth wide and get ready to receive!

Remember, you can see what you need to see. The pure in heart *see* God. When you are in your "Egypt," I AM is there with you and for you. His name *I AM* simply means "I will be what you need Me to be in your life." The greater works are in you. John 14:12 (AMP) says, "I assure you and most solemnly say to you, anyone who believes in Me [as Savior] will also do the things that I do; and he will do even greater things than these [in extent and outreach], because I am going to the Father."

> HOPE IS LIKE A ROPE; GRAB IT AND DON'T LET GO. YOUR FUTURE IS TIED TO YOUR EXPECTATIONS, AND YOUR EXPECTATIONS ARE INFLUENCED BY YOUR EMOTIONS. SUBDUE YOUR EMOTIONS AND THINK AS GOD DOES.

Chronicles of faith are still being written! "There are also many other things which Jesus did, which if they were recorded one by one, I suppose that even the world itself could not contain the books that would be written" (John 21:25, AMP). Your story is meant to join the record of faith in Hebrews 11. Remember, you can *see* if you want to *see* from His perspective.

You have "a future and a hope" (Jer. 29:11). Hope is like a rope; grab it and don't let go. Your future is tied to your expectations, and your expectations are influenced by your emotions. Subdue your emotions and think as God does. Feelings may challenge your faith, but look for God to do the unexpected. Expect God!

God assures both the body of Christ and the world that there is a future and a hope. By His Spirit I believe the Lord revealed that we will continue beyond 2026. He gave me a sense of certainty about that revelation, which means that He has much more in store.

So don't waste time—step into your place in His plan!

A PERSONAL INVITATION FROM THE AUTHOR

GOD LOVES YOU deeply. His Word is filled with promises that reveal His desire to bring healing, hope, and abundant life to every area of your being—body, mind, and spirit. More than anything He wants a personal relationship with you through His Son, Jesus Christ.

If you've never invited Jesus into your life, you can do so right now. It's not about religion; it's about a relationship with the One who knows you completely and loves you unconditionally. If you're ready to take that step, simply pray this prayer with a sincere heart:

Lord Jesus, I want to know You as my Savior and Lord. I confess and believe that You are the Son of God and that You died for my sins. I believe You rose from the dead and are alive today. Please forgive me for my sins. I invite You into my heart and my life. Make me new. Help me walk with You, grow in Your love, and live for You every day. In Jesus' name, amen.

If you just prayed that prayer, you have made the most important decision of your life. All of heaven is rejoicing with you, and I rejoice as well! You are now a child of God, beginning a new journey with Him.

To hear me personally share about what it means to follow Christ, scan the QR code on this page. I would be honored to guide you through the life-changing decision to accept Jesus and experience His love for yourself.

Please reach out to my publisher at pray4me@charismamedia. com if you accepted Jesus today or if this book has encouraged or impacted your life in any way. We'd love to celebrate with you and send you free materials to help strengthen your faith. We look forward to hearing from you!

chuckpiercebook.com/invitation

NOTES

Chapter 1

1. *Merriam-Webster*, "viewpoint," accessed June 13, 2024, https://www.merriam-webster.com/dictionary/viewpoint.
2. Etymonline, "perspective," accessed June 13, 2025, https://www.etymonline.com/search?q=perspective.
3. The "evil eye" can indicate many negative traits. "What Does the Evil Eye Mean?," Bible Hub, accessed June 13, 2025, https://biblehub.com/q/what_does_the_evil_eye_mean.htm.
4. R. Laird Harris et al., *Theological Wordbook of the Old Testament* (Moody Press, 1999), 650, under "*awa*."
5. Cindy Jacobs, *The Voice of God* (Regal Books, 1995), 64.
6. Jacobs, *The Voice of God*, 64.
7. For more on this, see Chuck D. Pierce, *The Passover Prophecies* (Charisma House, 2020).
8. Pierce, *The Passover Prophecies*, 19–20.

Chapter 2

1. Etymonline, "Peirce," accessed June 14, 2025, https://www.etymonline.com/word/Peirce.
2. "Ultimate Fast Facts Guide to Nuclear Energy," U.S. Department of Energy, January 2019, 4, https://www.energy.gov/sites/prod/files/2019/01/f58/Ultimate%20Fast%20Facts%20Guide-PRINT.pdf.
3. Chuck D. Pierce and Pamela J. Pierce, *One Thing* (Destiny Image, 2006).

Chapter 3

1. "DeLorean Time Machine," Futurepedia, accessed June 5, 2025, https://backtothefuture.fandom.com/wiki/DeLorean_Time_Machine.
2. PopKatsu, "George McFly—I Don't Know If I Could Take That Kind of Rejection … [Back to the Future] (1985)," YouTube, September 22, 2022, https://www.youtube.com/watch?v=oi4lw20xTCY.
3. Mendiant, "Back to the Future—That Kind of Rejection," YouTube, January 7, 2013, https://www.youtube.com/watch?v=eqwrUUAMrdY.

4. Blue Letter Bible, "*bādad*," accessed August 29, 2025, https://www.blueletterbible.org/lexicon/h909/nkjv/wlc/0-1/; James Swanson, *Dictionary of Biblical Languages with Semantic Domains: Hebrew (Old Testament)* (Logos Research Systems, 1997).
5. Google search results for "The Greek mindset did not perceive from the standpoint of time but from that of space and that which is concrete," Google, accessed July 1, 2025, https://www.google.com/search?q=The+Greek+mindset+did+not+perceive+from+the+standpoint+of+time+but+from+that+of+space+and+that+which+is+concrete.
6. Blue Letter Bible, "*bādad*"; Julian Sinclair, "Berachah," *Jewish Chronicle*, accessed June 6, 2025, https://www.thejc.com/judaism/jewish-words/berachah-h1pbkjxg.

CHAPTER 4

1. "Situational Thinking," *Mevakesh Lev*, July 24, 2018, https://mevakeshlev.blogspot.com/2018/07/situational-thinking.html.
2. "Situational Thinking," *Mevakesh Lev*.
3. Austin Burkhart, "'Avodah': What It Means to Live a Seamless Life of Work, Worship, and Service," Institute for Faith, Work and Economics, March 31, 2015, https://tifwe.org/avodah-a-life-of-work-worship-and-service/.

CHAPTER 5

1. Nife Oluyemi, "Expectations," Medium, February 3, 2017, https://nife.medium.com/expectations-2e8f16664e20.
2. "English Language and Usage," Stack Exchange, accessed June 6, 2025, https://english.stackexchange.com/questions/628821/whats-the-most-succinct-way-to-say-that-someone-feels-the-desire-to-do-somethin.
3. Sarah Pierce, personal communication, December 11, 2009.
4. Blue Letter Bible, "*tᵊšûqâ*," accessed June 6, 2025, https://www.blueletterbible.org/lexicon/h8669/nkjv/wlc/0-1/.
5. *Encarta World English Dictionary*, "expectation" (St. Martin's Press, 1999).
6. Bible Hub, "4328. Prosdokaó," accessed June 6, 2025, https://biblehub.com/greek/4328.htm.
7. Blue Letter Bible, "*apokaradokía*," accessed June 6, 2025, https://www.blueletterbible.org/lexicon/g603/kjv/tr/0-1/.
8. Devon Denomme, "Social Loafing: Definition, Effects, Prevention, and Examples," Study.com, accessed June 20, 2025, https://study.

com/learn/lesson/social_loafing_examples_effects_of_social_
loafing.html.

9. Hart et al., "Achievement Motivation, Expected Coworker Performance, and Collective Task Motivation: Working Hard or
Hardly Working?," *Journal of Applied Social Psychology 34*, no.
5 (2004): ," 994.

10. Hart et al., "Achievement Motivation," 990.

11. Hart et al., "Achievement Motivation," 984, 985, 991.

12. Hart et al., "Achievement Motivation," 994.

13. "Teacher Expectations Student Achievement," Mike McMahon
AUSD, accessed June, 7, 2025, https://www.mikemcmahon.info/
tesa.htm.

14. "Teacher Expectations," Mike McMahon AUSD.

15. "Teacher Expectations," Mike McMahon AUSD.

16. "Teacher Expectations," Mike McMahon AUSD.

17. Footnote in John 14:16–17 (TPT).

CHAPTER 6

1. Dave Hunt, *Peace, Prosperity, and the Coming Holocaust* (Harvest
House, 1983).

2. Joseph H. Hellerman, *The Ancient Church as Family* (Fortress
Press, 2001), 25.

3. Google search results for "process is the course or method of continuing development that involves change," Google, accessed July
3, 2025, https://www.google.com/search?q=process+is+the+course
+or+method+of+continuing+development+that+involves+change&
oq=process+is+the+course+or+method+of+continuing+developm-
ent+that+involves+change.

4. "Make School Easy with Brainly +," accessed June 23, 2025, https://
brainly.com/question/32422227.

5. Janice Swinney, personal communication, March 20, 2010.

CHAPTER 7

1. "U.S.–China Relations," Council on Foreign Relations, accessed
June 9, 2025, https://www.cfr.org/timeline/us-china-relations.

2. "China Country Report on Human Rights Practices for 1996," U.S.
Department of State, January 30, 1997, https://1997-2001.state.gov/
global/human_rights/1996_hrp_report/china.html.

3. "Postdenominational Church," Encyclopedia.com, accessed June 10,
2025, https://www.encyclopedia.com/religion/legal-and-political-
magazines/postdenominational-church.

4. Bill Hamon, *Apostles Prophets and the Coming Moves of God* (Destiny Image, 1997), 10.

5. Michael Elliott, "China Takes on the World," *Time*, January 11, 2007, https://time.com/archive/6596769/china-takes-on-the-world/.

6. Jacques deLisle, "Beijing's Olympic Moments, 2008 and 2022: How China and the Meaning of the Games Have, and Have Not, Changed," Foreign Policy Research Institute, February 3, 2022, https://www.fpri.org/article/2022/02/beijings-olympic-moments-2008-and-2022-how-china-and-the-meaning-of-the-games-have-and-have-not-changed.

7. Tao Wenzhao, "China-US Relations in 2016," China-US Focus, January 3, 2017, https://www.chinausfocus.com/foreign-policy/china-us-relations-in-2016.

8. Kevin Rudd, "The Avoidable War: Reflections on U.S.–China Relations and the End of Strategic Engagement," Asia Society Policy Institute, January 21, 2019, https://asiasociety.org/policy-institute/avoidable-war-reflections-us-china-relations-and-end-strategic-engagement.

CHAPTER 8

1. Dutch Sheets and Chuck D. Pierce, *Releasing the Prophetic Destiny of a Nation* (Destiny Image, 2005).

2. Tim Sheets, *The New Era of Glory* (Destiny Image, 2019).

3. After the Lord entered me into the writing of the book *The Future War of the Church* and showed me *God's Unfolding Battle Plan*, He revealed another book *A Time to Triumph*—three books you might read if you desire to go further into the Lord's call to His ecclesia. Later, Robert Heidler and I wrote two books: *The Apostolic Church Arising* and *A Triumphant Kingdom*. These books are helpful in giving you a complete vision of how God's kingdom is advancing in the earth.

4. Please note that there was no train station on Ellis Island. A terminal in Jersey City was used for immigrants who needed transportation on land. Mobile Instinct, "Ellis Island's Train Terminal Still Exists!" YouTube, March 13, 2024, https://www.youtube.com/watch?v=QGoOjuNaqJE.

5. Pierce, *Redeeming the Time*.

6. Pierce, *Redeeming the Time*, 146.

7. Pierce and Heidler, *Apostolic Church Arising*; Pierce, *Time to Triumph*.

8. Pierce, *Time to Triumph*, 166–167.

9. Stephen E. Strang, *God and Donald Trump* (FrontLine, 2017); Stephen E. Strang, *Trump Aftershock* (FrontLine, 2018); Stephen E. Strang, *God, Trump and the 2020 Election* (FrontLine, 2020).
10. Pierce, *The Passover Prophecies*, 109-110.
11. Lisa Lyons, personal communication, Dec. 11, 2024.
12. Pierce, *The Passover Prophecies*, 110-111.
13. Pierce, *The Passover Prophecies*, 111-113.
14. Josef Federman and Tia Goldenberg, "Israeli Supreme Court: Netanyahu May Form Government," AP, May 6, 2020, https://apnews.com/article/24b186bf96fd3a97e3e0e814fc10fcf7.

CHAPTER 9

1. *Websters Dictionary 1828, American Dictionary of the English Language*, "decree," accessed July 4, 2025, https://webstersdictionary1828.com/Dictionary/decree.
2. Dutch Sheets and Chuck Pierce, "15 Prophetic Decrees to Dismantle Darkness and Release Miracles in America," Destiny Image, July 24, 2024, https://www.destinyimage.com/blog/dutch-sheets-chuck-pierce-15-prophetic-decrees-to-dismantle-darkness-and-release-miracles-in-america.
3. Deuteronomy 33:29 says, "Your enemies shall submit to you, and you shall tread down their high places." High places in the Bible are often linked with places of sin and iniquity, places of idolatrous altars. We all have or have had high places in our lives filled with sin and iniquity, sometimes even passed down to us through the generations. The power of God through the Holy Spirit gives us the ability to tread down the high places and defeat old enemies living there. This overcoming power allows God to break our conformity to the standards of this world and renew our minds. He is able to replace old deceptions that have caused us to fail in the past with a new belief system that will bring us to success.
4. Linda Heidler, personal communication, December 19, 2024.
5. Chuck D. Pierce and Alemu Beeftu, *The King's Signet Ring* (Baker Books, 2022).
6. *Merriam-Webster*, "shift," accessed June 11, 2025, https://www.merriam-webster.com/dictionary/shift.
7. *Merriam-Webster*, "shift."
8. Collins Dictionary, "schism," accessed June 12, 2025, https://www.collinsdictionary.com/us/dictionary/english/schism.
9. *Merriam-Webster*, "rift," accessed June 12, 2025, https://www.merriam-webster.com/dictionary/rift.

10. "Our Relationship," U.S. Embassy in Ukraine, accessed June 11, 2025, https://ua.usembassy.gov/our-relationship/.

11. Lisa Lyons, personal communication, August 21, 2024.

ACKNOWLEDGMENTS

THANK YOU TO all those who have helped me keep clear perspective, especially Pam Pierce and Brian Kooiman.

ABOUT THE AUTHOR

CHARLES D. "CHUCK" Pierce leads an apostolic and prophetic ministry in Corinth, Texas, as president of Glory of Zion International and Kingdom Harvest Alliance. These ministries are housed at Global Spheres Center, which is also home to Beulah Acres and the Israel Prayer Garden. The ministries located at Global Spheres Center participate in regional and national gatherings to develop new kingdom paradigms.

Dr. Pierce gathers and mobilizes the worshipping Triumphant Reserve throughout the world and serves as a key bridge between Jew and Gentile as the Lord raises up "one new man." He is known for his accurate prophetic gifting, which helps direct nations, cities, churches, and individuals in understanding the times and seasons in which we live. He has written numerous best-selling books and has a degree in business from Texas A&M University, a master's in cognitive systems from the University of North Texas, and a DMin from Wagner University.

To learn more about his ministry, visit gloryofzion.org.

linktr.ee/gziministries

No More Boring Bible Study offers a faithful and fresh perspective on studying God's Word. Faith's guidance is like that of a caring sister: informed, relatable, and affirming. This book will develop a new hunger for studying the Bible and equip you with the tools you need to satisfy it.

–KAELIN AND KYRAH EDWARDS,
authors, *This Kind of Love*

No More Boring Bible Study is a book that every Christian should read, consume, and apply. Faith breaks down the exact strategies you need to go from surface-level Bible reading to deeper Bible *study*. After reading this book, you'll have a clear roadmap for how to study the Scriptures, hear from God yourself, and, most important, experience change. Get one copy for yourself and give another to a friend.

–ALLEN PARR, ThM, Christian YouTuber, *The BEAT;*
founder, Let's Equip, Inc.; author, *Misled*

Faith Womack loves God and his Word, and she'll help you do the same. *No More Boring Bible Study* offers an accessible overview of both why and how we read the Bible. You'll gain the tools you need for a lifetime of rich and fruitful time in God's Word.

–COURTNEY DOCTOR, director of women's initiatives,
The Gospel Coalition; Bible teacher; author, *From Garden
to Glory, In View of God's Mercies,* and others

If you want to go from a Bible Newb to a Bible Nerd, this book can help. Faith Womack's passion for studying the Bible is contagious, and *No More Boring Bible Study* will help anyone who struggles with the Bible become a more engaged student of Scripture.

–TIM WILDSMITH, author, *Bible Translations
for Everyone* and *Daily Scripture Guidebook*

If you have wanted to understand your Bible better but felt intimidated by it, assuming that it's only for the professionals, this book is for you. Faith loves God, she loves Scripture, and she is passionate about helping others discover the wonder of the Bible. This book is welcoming, wise, and winsome.

—**KELLY M. KAPIC,** professor of theological studies, Covenant College; author, *You're Only Human*

Faith's joy for God's Word is contagious. With heartfelt stories, rich biblical truth, and a touch of her bubbly personality, this book makes Bible study feel like a coffee date with a wise and fun friend: deep, delightful, and anything but boring.

—**ASHLEY ARMIJO,** Coffee and Bible Time

Faith Womack has an abundance of personality, and it shines through on every page of *No More Boring Bible Study.* Her wit and wisdom, put in down-to-earth, pithy sayings, fill the book. I found myself highlighting sentence after sentence.

This slender volume has surprising depth and breadth. Faith has the ability to communicate a great amount of rich material that even a preteen can understand. She has distilled major academic works on studying the Bible in plain (but not boring) English. And Faith delights her readers with mini Bible studies throughout. Her love for God's Word is infectious. She lets the reader into her world, complete with her frustrations and flaws, humor and humility, to see vivid illustrations of the chapter's lessons.

If you want to get serious about studying the Bible and want an approach that is anything but boring, this is the book for you.

—**DANIEL B. WALLACE,** senior research professor emeritus, New Testament studies, Dallas Theological Seminary; CEO and executive director, Center for the Study of New Testament Manuscripts